CINEMA
SEX
SIRENS

Copyright © 2011 Omnibus Press
(A Division of Music Sales Limited)

Cover designed by Paul Tippett for Vitamin P
Book designed by Paul Tippett and Adrian Andrews for Vitamin P
Picture research by Dave Worrall, Lee Pfeiffer and Jacqui Black

Hardcover edition:
ISBN: 978.1.84938.994.5
Order No: OP54032

Softcover edition:
ISBN: 978.1.78038.184.8
Order No: OP54351

Exclusive Distributors
Music Sales Limited,
14/15 Berners Street,
London, W1T 3LJ.

Music Sales Corporation,
257 Park Avenue South,
New York, NY 10010, USA.

Macmillan Distribution Services,
56 Parkwest Drive
Derrimut, Vic 3030,
Australia.

Every effort has been made to trace the copyright holders of the photographs in this book
but one or two were unreachable. We would be grateful if the photographers concerned
would contact us.

Printed in China.

A catalogue record for this book is available from the British Library.

Visit Omnibus Press on the web at www.omnibuspress.com

CINEMA
Sex
SIRENS

DAVE WORRALL & LEE PFEIFFER

OMNIBUS PRESS

CONTENTS

6
Foreword:
Sir Roger Moore

8
Introduction

10
Hollywood or Bust:
The Early Years

16 PART 1:
...and Hollywood
Created the
Sex Symbol

20
Raquel Welch

26
Ann-Margret

28
Carroll Baker

30
The Russ Meyer
Ladies

32
Angie Dickinson

34
Jane Fonda

38
Janet Leigh

40
Jill St John

42
Drive-in Gals

44
Stella Stevens

46
Sharon Tate

50
Mamie Van Doren

52
Natalie Wood

56
Blaxploitation!

60 PART 2:
The Continentals

62
Ursula Andress

66
Brigitte Bardot

72
Senta Berger

74
Claudia Cardinale

78
Anita Ekberg

82 Britt Ekland

84 Giallo Girls

88 Sylva Koscina

90 Sylvia Kristel

94 Gina Lollobrigida

98 Sophia Loren

104 Luciana Paluzzi

106 Elke Sommer

108 Barbara Steele

110 The Continentals Round-up

118 PART 3:
Made in England: Brit Glamour

126 Susan George

128 Suzy Kendall

130 Valerie Leon

132 Helen Mirren

134 Caroline Munro

136 Ingrid Pitt

138 Madeline Smith

140 Brit Glamour Round-up

148 Sex Sells: The Art of the Movie Poster

159 Bibliography
About the Authors

FOREWORD

Some years ago when I wore a halo and pretended to be *The Saint*, I was interviewed for a British television programme where the illustrious host kicked off by saying:

"As Ivanhoe, Maverick and Simon Templar, you've worked your way through your fair share of leading ladies…" Nearly choking, I interrupted and replied, "You can't say that!" Not quite appreciating my objection, the director said, "Okay, let's go again. Take two." "As Ivanhoe, Maverick and now Simon Templar, you've got through quite a lot of leading ladies in your time…"

I burst out laughing. He honestly didn't realise quite what he was saying. However, if he had said I had been lucky to share the screen with a number of terrific actresses in my career, then I would have agreed whole-heartedly.

From Hollywood to Elstree and Pinewood studios in England, I have appeared alongside many of the ladies featured in this book. My only grumble is that they are all far prettier than me. I duly took my revenge by playing all manner of silly jokes on them and, worst of all, I smoked. Can you imagine filming a love scene, with all of the passion and desire the script calls for, when your leading man moves in for a kiss and all you get is a terrible whiff of cigar smoke on his breath? Yuck! I apologise to them all for forcing them to kiss a walking ashtray.

I have now stopped smoking, and as long as I don't enjoy it too much my wife Kristina says she will understand if my next film calls for a love scene. I await the scripts with anticipation.

Sir Roger Moore
Monaco, February 2011

Above: By 1961, Roger Moore had gained third-billing status in *The Sins of Rachel Cade*, seen here with actress Angie Dickinson, who played the titular role.
Opposite: Roger Moore as the suave and sophisticated Simon Templar poses with a bevy of beauties, as well as the now classic Volvo sports car, on the studio backlot during the filming of an episode of the hit TV show *The Saint*. During a seven-year period, 116 one-hour episodes were shown in over 80 countries and made the actor internationally famous.

INTRODUCTION

"They don't make 'em like they used to!" That time-worn cliché has frequently been used by retro movie lovers to decry the current state of today's motion picture industry. It is also applicable to the stars.

One can make a cogent argument that contemporary actors are more diverse than those who populated the industry in decades gone by. It might be said that actors like Leonardo DiCaprio and Natalie Portman have a far wider range than John Wayne or Marilyn Monroe… but when was the last time you were inspired to pluck a random DiCaprio or Portman film off the shelf and indulge in the sheer pleasure of watching them, the way you would with the more legendary stars? As the publishers of *Cinema Retro* magazine, which celebrates movies of the 1960s and 1970s, we're often accused of giving short-shrift to contemporary motion pictures. In fact, there are still some great ones being made – but for every *The King's Speech,* one must wade through an unpleasant morass of over-hyped monstrosities based on action figures, amusement park rides and Burger King toys.

Nowhere is the decline of glamour in today's films as evident as in the dearth of truly exotic leading ladies. True, the Oscar and BAFTA ceremonies can still be counted on to provide a periodic glimpse into what was once a routine aspect of the industry (i.e. women dressed to the nines, sashaying down a red carpet). However, for true glamour, one must revisit a bygone era. Commencing with the early days of motion pictures and extending through to the mid-Sixties, studios often placed actresses and actors under exclusive contract. These agreements were usually long term and subjected the artists to the whims of studio bosses. One of the requirements for actresses was the mandatory attendance at schools of etiquette, where young women were taught how to dress, walk, talk and engage in aspects of grooming designed to make them appear like goddesses on the silver screen.

By today's standards, these practices seem ridiculously quaint and highly sexist. And indeed they were. However, the women who emerged from this system were the epitome of taste and glamour. Perhaps that is why we now see such a fanatical craving for films from these eras. Certainly, much of the success of the Sixties-based TV drama series *Mad Men* can be attributed to the presentation of the women on the show. This was a period when women wore stockings and suspenders, bras that resembled barrage balloons and had hips and breasts that could *only* be described as 'voluptuous'. Yes, the celebration of curves was king (or should that be queen?) and actresses were either exploited by the studio system, or chose to exploit themselves to enhance their reputation at the box office. Some dared, some bared. Some disappeared into obscurity, and some became famous. But the one common denominator was the fact that they had all earned the moniker 'sex sirens'.

It's difficult to say precisely when real glamour disappeared from society, but we believe we can pinpoint the culprit responsible: Mr Ernest G. Rice. "Who?", you may ask. Mr Rice was the man widely credited with making pantyhose an international sensation in the 1960s. In doing so, garter belts and stockings, once routine fashion accessories, were replaced with a far more practical and comfortable substitute. And whilst he may have earned the thanks of millions of women worldwide, he simultaneously incurred the wrath of nearly all heterosexual males and struck a blow against cinematic eroticism. Can you imagine, for instance, *The Graduate*'s Mrs Robinson being the almost mythical siren she is if we had observed her seducing young Benjamin by wiggling out of a pair of pantyhose? Today, we may have unlimited porn only a mouse click away, but vulgarity can't replace genuine sensuality. When Bogie and Bacall used a discussion of racehorses as a thinly veiled euphemism for sex in Howard Hawks' *The Big Sleep* (1946), there was more titillation than in a dozen explicit feature films. Similarly, what image in film today can compare with the iconic movie poster photo of Sue Lyon 'innocently' sucking on a lollipop in *Lolita* (1962)?

Within these pages is a celebration of the great sex sirens of cinema's 1960s and 1970s heyday. The photos represent another bygone era of motion picture art, when meticulously crafted publicity shots were the norm. Such photos barely exist in today's industry, where only a handful of images are made available to publicise a current movie. Few, if any, exhibit the skills that are apparent in these glorious artifacts, representative of a time when glamour reigned over the motion picture industry.

We have, however, also taken pains to illustrate that there was much more to the ladies we honour than merely their physical assets. As their biographies indicate, these women had to overcome the casting-couch system as well as the public perception that if they were busty, they couldn't be brainy. In fact, these ladies used their intellect and business savvy to not only survive, but to thrive in an environment that was often demeaning to their self esteem. The fact that even the least-known among them still has a loyal following today is proof of their success. We hope that you enjoy this tribute to their talents and legacies. We think that even Mr Ernest G. Rice might be impressed.

Dave Worrall and Lee Pfeiffer
February 2011

Opposite: Voted *Esquire*'s Sexiest Woman in the World in 2010, the head-turning Christina Hendricks, who plays Joan Holloway in the Emmy-winning television show *Mad Men*, defines the term Sex Siren to voluptuous perfection.

HOLLYWOOD OR BUST: THE EARLY YEARS

While *Cinema Sex Sirens* is primarily a celebration of the female form as seen in movies from the Sixties and Seventies, we must also acknowledge the era that was responsible for creating the 'pin-up' on both the printed page and the cinema screen.

Since the invention of moving pictures sexy women have played their part in entertaining and titillating audiences the world over. One has only to look at the early naturist, horror, sci-fi and jungle adventure film posters that were adorned with buxom women in perilous situations to see how the female form was used to lure (predominantly) male audiences into cinemas. Whatever the theme, movie posters always made sure there was a young woman, usually in tight-fitting attire, as the main element of the design!

As early as 1932 Claudette Colbert appeared topless in Cecil B. DeMille's *The Sign of the Cross*, but it was in the late Thirties and early Forties that studio executives really began to turn their female stars into objects of desire, creating a clearly defined sexual image for many of their actresses. Whatever their attributes, be it long legs or large breasts, the studio photographers got to work on exploiting these women's physical charms. The impact was phenomenal, and photographs of actresses in provocative poses soon adorned magazine covers by their thousands. Not only were these women becoming household names, but their films were being heavily promoted, much to the delight of the studio bosses who immediately cashed in on this new found marketing tool. Many photographs – which were deemed risqué

at that time – were of women either showing their stocking-clad legs, or displaying an ample portion of cleavage in a low-cut dress or tight-fitting top. However, it was also an era of sturdy censorship, so nudity was taboo.

Since the early 1930s, the movie industry had been trying to stave off government censorship by adhering to its own strict guidelines known as the Hays Code, so named after the Presbyterian churchman who administered it and who thus became the chief arbiter of all things sexual in the cinema. Consequently, the Hays Code ensured that virtually all depictions of sex on screen were either eliminated or, at best, severely watered down. (The Code enforcers even took pains to make it clear that Rick and Ilsa never indulged in premarital relations in *Casablanca*!). Even properties where sex had been an integral part of their success, either on stage or the printed page, such as *A Streetcar Named Desire* (1951) and *From Here to Eternity* (1953), were significantly watered down when transferred to the big screen. The studios therefore had to be more creative in their development of female sex symbols and, increasingly, it became of paramount importance for an actress to suggest sexual passion with a mere look or gesture.

While it remained fashionable in the Thirties to be tall and slim like the flat-chested flapper girl of the previous decade, Hollywood's influence was about to change this trend. Lana Turner was given the nickname 'The Sweater Girl' after wearing form-fitting clothing in the movie *They Won't Forget* (1937) and the term soon became synonymous with any actress whose tight-fitting sweater emphasised a well-formed bust. By the Forties, movie glamour queens, like Betty Grable, Rhonda Fleming, Rita Hayworth and Ava Gardner, were being displayed in photos on the mess walls of soldiers fighting in World War Two, torn from the pages of magazines.

The age of the pin-up was upon us. However, these ladies were serious actresses too, willing to use a hint of their sexuality to promote their films, but they did not venture further into 'glamour girl' – women who *did* pose in as little clothing as possible – territory.

Opposite top: Nicknamed The Blonde Bombshell – and it's easy to see why! Jean Harlow in *Platinum Blonde* (1931).

Opposite below left: Made before the days of screen censorship, a naked Claudette Colbert bathes in asses' milk in Cecil B. DeMille's *The Sign of the Cross*, which caused a storm at the box-office – and a stink in the studio when the powdered cow's milk turned sour during the three days it took to film this scene.

Opposite right: Typical studio publicity shot of Betty Grable, who was known for having the most beautiful legs in Hollywood and famously had them insured by Lloyds of London for $1,000,000. A 1943 photograph of her in a swimsuit became GI's favourite pin-up shot during World War II.

Above: Discovered in a Los Angeles drug store aged just 16, Lana Turner's story is Hollywood legend. Remembered as the original Sweater Girl, a nickname earnt by her form-fitting clothing in her first film *They Won't Forget* as illustrated here, she was a popular pin-up girl during the Thirties and Forties.

Left: It all started here. American GIs relax in their barrack room, their walls adorned with photographs of glamorous actresses torn from the pages of magazines that they pinned to the wall. Hence the term 'pin-up'.

Although Fay Wray had appeared scantily clad in *King Kong* (1933), and stars like Mae West and Jean Harlow were notoriously sexual in their films and publicity, it was really the appearance of Jane Russell in Howard Hughes' *The Outlaw* (1943) which caused the greatest storm. Russell was signed to a seven-year contract by Hughes, who went to great lengths to showcase her voluptuous figure in his film about Billy the Kid. And it was this emphasis on Russell's well-endowed bust that resulted in the notorious censorship problems *The Outlaw* encountered. The film's whole advertising campaign was based around Russell's chest size, to the extent that the Motion Picture Association even considered Hughes' expulsion on a charge of violating the standards of good taste. The film was finally released in 1946, by which time Russell was well known across America – more for her 38D bust and the trouble it had caused than for her talents as an actress – so she got top billing on the posters, even though it was her first movie! She soon proved that her talents were greater than her figure and starred alongside Frank Sinatra, Robert Mitchum and Clark Gable during the early Fifties, with one of her most memorable films being *Gentlemen Prefer Blondes* (1953) opposite that other sex siren of the period, Marilyn Monroe.

Opposite: The smouldering look of a soon-to-be superstar: Jane Russell in *The Outlaw*.
Right: Jane Russell displays her more than ample charms as she poses for the painting to be used in *The Outlaw*'s ad campaign. It's pretty obvious what the film's main assets were.
Below: The marketing department took full advantage of Rita Heyworth's finer points when designing this poster for *Affair in Trinidad* (1952). Who wants to see Glenn Ford anyway?

Monroe, whose persona wasn't as sexually assertive as Russell's, was usually cast in either vulnerable roles or as the woman who would send men crazy without even realising it herself. Originally a brunette, Norma Jeane Dougherty (her married name at the time) was advised by her modeling agency to dye her hair 'golden' blonde in line with the current popularity of actresses like Betty Grable and Lana Turner. By the mid-Forties, and now divorced, she was offered a six-month contract with 20th Century Fox, where executive Ben Lyon suggested she change her name. She chose her mother's maiden name, which was Monroe, to which Lyon added 'Marilyn' – and a star was born.

During the early Fifties, a nude photograph of her taken in 1949, which she had posed when she had no money for rent, appeared on a calendar. The calendar caused quite a stir amongst the studio execs, who worried that it would hurt her reputation as an actress, but the controversy soon blew over and Marilyn gained work in films like *Clash by Night* (1952), before landing her first major role when Darryl F. Zanuck cast her in *Niagara* (1953). Much was

made of her sexuality in this film and many critics thought her 'personal' appearances were acts of pure vulgarity, mainly due to the outfits she wore. When she was chosen for the Grand Marshall at the Miss America Parade in September 1952, Marilyn chose to wear a dress with a neckline cut to her navel. It caused a furore, but the image was chosen for the first-ever cover of *Playboy* magazine in December 1953, which also featured the now-famous naked calendar shot inside. During her short-lived career, Marilyn Monroe was as famous for her private life as she was for her film appearances. Three marriages, a dalliance with the Kennedy family and a notoriety for being awkward on set all added to her mystique. Her most famous roles were probably in Billy Wilder's *The Seven Year Itch* (1955) and *Some Like It Hot* (1959), although Monroe made 30 films. She was found dead in her home on August 5, 1962, aged just 36, from a drug overdose.

While Marilyn Monroe was a 'one of a kind', Hollywood inevitably created many wannabees. Critics can debate whether Monroe was simply

in the right place at the right time, and discuss if her physical attributes contributed to her now-iconic status more than her acting ability. However, the same questions cannot be asked of the era's other well-known 'sex sirens' who appeared in the wake of Monroe's success: Jayne Mansfield and Mamie Van Doren *were* only known for their bodily charms. Although both have played their part in Hollywood history, they lacked Monroe's wonderful on-screen presence. Mansfield and Van Doren's main claim to fame was the size of their breasts and they were prepared to exploit their sexuality to the hilt. Both can really only be regarded as B-movie queens, but they nevertheless epitomise the phrase 'sex siren'!

As the Fifties came to a close, a new era of the 'sex siren' was about to unfold. The motion picture industry was in competition with television and needed to fight back with something TV could not provide. As in the past, the studios turned to the female form, but this time it would be bigger than ever.

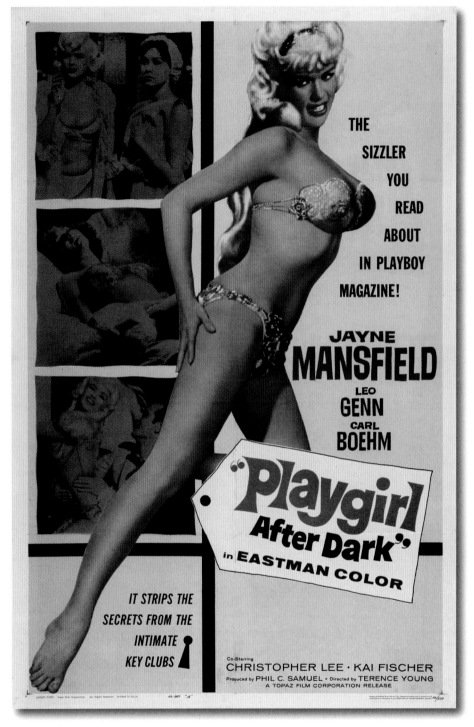

THE
SIZZLER
YOU
READ
ABOUT
IN PLAYBOY
MAGAZINE!

JAYNE
MANSFIELD
LEO
GENN
CARL
BOEHM

"Playgirl
After Dark"
in EASTMAN COLOR

IT STRIPS THE
SECRETS FROM THE
INTIMATE
KEY CLUBS

Co-Starring
CHRISTOPHER LEE · KAI FISCHER
Produced by PHIL C. SAMUEL · Directed by TERENCE YOUNG
A TOPAZ FILM CORPORATION RELEASE

Opposite: If this picture could talk, it would say, "come to bed with me." Could any man resist the gaze of a woman like Marilyn Monroe, seen here on the set of Billy Wilder's classic, *Some Like it Hot?*
Top left: Who said pole dancing was a new form of sexual entertainment? Marilyn Monroe publicity shot from *Let's Make Love* (1960).
Above left: The ever-alluring Gloria Grahame – seen hereon the set of *Naked Alibi* (1954) with director Jerry Hopper.
Above and left: *Too Hot to Handle* (1960) was notorious in its day due to Mansfield's risqué see-through clothing and its raunchy musical numbers. Made in Britain, and directed by Terence Young, who went on to helm the first James Bond film *Dr No*, the controversy held up the film's American release for two years. During this period *Playboy* magazine ran sexy images from the film, which was eventually released there as *Playgirl After Dark* (1962).

...AND HOLLYWOOD CREATED THE SEX SYMBOL

By the early 1960s, Hollywood was daring to take on such controversial subject matters as racism, sexual deviancy and drug use. The Hays Code was increasingly considered both restrictive and outdated, resulting in more and more directors pushing the envelope when it came to defying censorship.

Not surprisingly, the next generation of actresses to emerge from the Hollywood 'Dream Machine' reflected the audience's desire for realism. Suddenly, it was possible for an actress to achieve stardom on the merits of their talents, rather than their looks. Sex on screen was more realistically depicted and, while there was still room for glamour queens, there was now an emphasis on actresses with whom audiences could empathise.

Thus, women like Shirley MacLaine and Joanne Woodward became household names. Stunning beauties like Jane Fonda would play girl-next-door types, generally trying valiantly (but not too valiantly) to maintain their virginity against an onslaught of handsome suitors. Even

legendary screen beauty Elizabeth Taylor became frumpy and overweight for *Who's Afraid of Virginia Woolf?* (1966) – and won an Oscar despite being virtually unrecognisable. It was this film, with its adult depiction of sexual situations and language, that rendered the Hays Code obsolete. The Code was finally replaced by the current ratings system, initiated by the Motion Picture Association of America in 1968, which unleashed an explosion of creative freedom in American movies. Naturally, many of those films capitalised (sometimes pretentiously) on sexual scenarios that would have been considered obscene only a few years before. Actresses were suddenly asked to exploit their natural assets and, consequently, nude (or

near nude) scenes became almost obligatory for the new generation of female stars.

Above Donna Michelle in *One Spy Too Many*.
Below: The battle of the busts: Jayne Mansfield upstages Sophia Loren at Romanoff's restaurant in Beverley Hills in 1957. During a party for Loren, Mansfield pulled off a publicity stunt whereby one of her nipples was exposed, thus ensuring her photograph was published worldwide. Loren was not amused.
Opposite: Pausing between takes on *Giant* (1956), Elizabeth Taylor was often cast as a sexual firebrand capable of seducing her on-screen characters and audiences alike. Men wanted her, and women wanted to be like her. There are few actresses who will ever achieve the greatness of this Hollywood legend.

Above left: In one of cinema's sexiest moments, Lucille (Joy Harmon) suggestively washed a car in front of a group of sex-starved convicts in *Cool Hand Luke*. Measuring a stunning 41-22-36, Harmon retired from acting to open her own bakery in California!

Above right: Cheesecake studio publicity still of Edy Williams in *Good Times* (1967). Williams was a model whose film career was based on her bust size, not her acting ability. She was also noted for being married to soft-porn king Russ Meyer.

Right: Yvonne Craig in *The Man From U.N.C.L.E.* big-screen adventure *One of Our Spies is Missing* (1966). The films were made from two TV episodes, with extra footage featuring sexy girls added to appeal to the adult audiences who were also flocking to see the James Bond films at that time.

Far right: Julie Newmar, who appeared in countless Sixties TV shows – and posed nude for the May 1968 issue of *Playboy* – is best remembered for her role as Catwoman in the hit TV show *Batman*.

Opposite: Although known for her acting, singing and dancing, Shirley MacLaine also added a touch of glamour to the usually all-macho world of the Clint Eastwood Western, playing the titular role in *Two Mules For Sister Sara* (1970).

While some might argue that the Sixties turned actresses into sexual objects, it is also true that women could nevertheless achieve stardom upon talent alone. Anne Bancroft, for example, would never have made it as a sex kitten in the 1940s or 1950s, but she gained screen immortality as the original cougar, Mrs Robinson, in the 1967 film *The Graduate*. Still, the studios were not in the business of propagating women's liberation. Sex was selling like never before and Hollywood executives still went to great pains to create and market the next great sex symbol.

There is, perhaps, no greater example of how an actress can be built into a marketable brand than Raquel Welch. Signed under exclusive contract to Fox in the mid-Sixties, the studio realised that the statuesque beauty had a potential that went far beyond the usual flash-in-the-pan sex symbols. The Hammer Films production *One Million Years B.C.* (1966) used her as the focus of its main ad campaign, although Welch's previous film, the acclaimed *Fantastic Voyage* (1966), had offered scant opportunities to capitalise on her sex appeal.

Welch soon became a major star, alternating between quality films like *Bandolero!* (1968) and action movies like *Fathom* (1967) and *Flareup* (1969), which seemed to exist purely to exploit her sex appeal.

Similarly, Ursula Andress, who made screen history with her white bikini in the first James Bond film *Dr. No* (1962), also found her physical beauty being used as her films' key selling point. Other actresses, who never quite reached the same levels of stardom, seemed content to co-operate with studio strategies to use images of their physical attributes to help promote movies. In most cases, they were given supporting roles in films purely to provide a sex appeal angle in publicity photos and marketing materials. However, some did gain a legitimate fan base. Both Julie Newmar and Yvonne Craig found loyal followings playing Catwoman and Batgirl respectively on the *Batman* TV series. Others, such as Sharon Tate, soon landed quality roles in major studio productions, while actresses like Edy Williams clearly embraced sexual exploitation and proudly built an entire career around such a strategy. Some also went

on to fame, though not fortune, simply on the basis of one memorable screen role. Joy Harmon still has a fervent fan following today based solely on her brief, wordless role as a scantily clad young woman who is seen washing a car in *Cool Hand Luke* (1967).

By the 1970s, times were beginning to change, as societal attitudes shifted and the women's liberation movement continued to grow. Overt emphasis on an actress's physical attributes still existed, but was beginning to seem a little outdated. The new freedoms did, however, also bring about the era of the blaxploitation film, in which actresses like Pam Grier and Tamara Dobson clearly emulated the marketing techniques of the prior decade. By the decade's end, in mainstream Hollywood films, studios largely developed and sold stars based on their acting ability – although the occasional throwback to a more glamorous earlier period did sometimes appear, as evidenced by Bo Derek's pop-icon status following her appearance in the 1979 film *10*.

2029-87

RAQUEL WELCH

One of the screen's most enduring sex symbols, Raquel Welch has always radiated class and style. She has generally played women with courage and dignity, and quickly proved to the film industry that she was far more than the flash-in-the-pan beauty that many people predicted she would be.

Welch was born in Chicago in 1940 as Jo Raquel Tejeda. Her father was an immigrant from Bolivia who became an aeronautical engineer. Her mother, a native-born American, traced her ancestry back to the *Mayflower*. Despite her impressive background, Welch struggled to achieve success. She married at age 18 to James Welch and kept his name even after the marriage dissolved. She got her first taste of fame by working as a weather girl on a TV station in San Diego, California, before relocating to Texas with her two young children.

Here, Welch got some modeling contracts, but still had to moonlight in unglamorous jobs to make ends meet. Frustrated, but well aware of her good looks, Welch moved back to California, this time to Hollywood where she was determined to find work in show business. She had bit parts in popular TV series and landed a few minor roles in the feature films *A House is Not a Home* (1964), *Roustabout*

(1964) with Elvis Presley, and *A Swingin' Summer* (1965).

Astute studio executives at Fox recognised that Welch's stunning looks and spectacular body could form the basis of exploitation ad campaigns. The studio signed her to an exclusive contract, even though this practice had virtually been phased out by this point. Curiously, Welch's first film for Fox did not in any way exploit her physical attributes. *Fantastic Voyage* (1966) told of a team of scientists who are miniaturised and injected into a man's body in order to save his life, and therefore featured little opportunity to show much skin, since Welch was mostly clad in a scuba suit. However, a teaser poster, which featured her totally naked and was in no way connected to the movie, fully exploited her obvious charms!

The film was a substantial hit and Fox next loaned Welch out to Hammer Films in England for a true exploitation classic, the 1966 remake

of *One Million Years B.C.* Hammer wasn't about to ignore Welch's beauty and it could be argued that the sole reason for the movie's existence was to allow her to run about amongst the dinosaurs whilst clad only in a fur bikini. Critics scoffed, but the film was a major hit – thanks in no small part to a creative ad campaign featuring an image of Welch which quickly became one of the Sixties most iconic photographs. Reflecting back on the image during a 2010 interview with *The Guardian*, Welch said: "I knew I wasn't that sexy woman in the picture. I might have looked it, but I didn't feel it. After all, what nobody was supposed to know was that I was divorced, the mother of two young children, and alone in a man's world."

Top: *Hannie Caulder.*
Below right: Publicity contact sheet from *Fantastic Voyage.*
Opposite: Posing for publicity in-between filming *Fathom.*

Above: The film that started the journey to stardom: *One Million Years B.C.*.

Above top right: Bikini power. Japanese poster art for *Fathom*.

Above middle right: Welch's fur bikini was the main selling point of *One Million Years B.C.* and appeared on magazine covers world-wide.

Right: Welch starred as 'Lust' in the comedy *Bedazzled*, a retelling of the Faust legend set in swinging Sixties London, written by and starring Peter Cook and Dudley Moore.

Many predicted that Welch's career would quickly burn out, as had been the fate of so many other actresses who had been proclaimed 'The Next Big Thing'. However, she proved to have staying power and, more importantly, acting ability. Welch was perfectly cast as Lust in the cult Peter Cook and Dudley Moore comedy *Bedazzled* (1967) and Fox also began starring her with the era's top name talent. She was seen opposite Dean Martin and James Stewart in *Bandolero!* (1968) and the same year showed considerable charisma on-screen with Frank Sinatra in *Lady in Cement*, a sequel to Sinatra's gumshoe hit *Tony Rome*, which had been released the previous year.

The fact that she acquitted herself well opposite such heavyweight talents brought some respect from the critical establishment, even if much of it was grudging and condescending. In 1969, a Welch film set off a firestorm of controversy when she co-starred with Jim Brown in the Western *100 Rifles*. In an era where inter-racial romance was still taboo in the recently integrated American South, the film was deemed provocative – especially since it poked racists in the eye with a poster of Welch draping her arms around a bare-chested Brown.

Throughout the 1970s Welch's star continued to rise, despite having a starring role opposite the legendary Mae West in the disastrous all-star screen adaptation of Gore Vidal's *Myra Breckinridge* (1970). She won plaudits for her performance as a revenge-driven rape victim in the 1971 Western *Hannie Caulder*, starred opposite up-and-comer Burt Reynolds in the comedy *Fuzz* (1972) and gained excellent notices for her role in the roller derby drama *Kansas City Bomber* (1972). Welch also received praise for her comic performances in *The Three Musketeers* (1973) and *The Four Musketeers* (1974). Additionally, she appeared in the acclaimed all-star comedy/mystery *The Last of Sheila* (1973). Welch proved she could deftly play light comedy as well as drama and widened her audience with a TV special called *Raquel!* that featured her performing with such diverse talents as Tom Jones and John Wayne. Alas, age-based discrimination has always been rampant in Hollywood and Welch suffered an embarrassment in 1981 when MGM fired her from a screen adaptation of Steinbeck's *Cannery Row* because the studio felt she was too old to be a credible love interest. Welch, who was 40 at the time, successfully sued and was awarded a multi-million dollar settlement.

Against all odds, Welch's career continued to thrive, largely because she diversified her projects. She made other TV specials and earned praise for her work in two acclaimed TV movies, *The Legend of Walks Far Woman* (1982) and *Right to Die* (1987). Welch followed Jane Fonda's lead and launched a fitness programme that became the basis of a best-selling book. She also created a successful nightclub act that accentuated her talents for singing and dancing. Plus she had successful runs on Broadway in *Woman of the Year* and *Victor/Victoria*.

In the 1990s, Welch proved she could spoof her own image, playing a diva in an episode of *Seinfeld*. She has continued to be a regular presence in the public eye through high-profile commercials for cosmetics and Foster Grant sunglasses, the latter fully capitalising on her legendary sex appeal. In 2010, she wrote her autobiography, which looked back philosophically on her career and survival after four failed marriages. The title was, appropriately enough, *Raquel: Beyond the Cleavage*.

Top left: The coupling of Welch and Jim Brown in *100 Rifles* was considered a daring and brave decision in Hollywood at that time, despite the increasing popularity of films featuring black actors. It was one of the first mainstream films to feature an interracial sex scene.

Top right: A cameo role in *The Magic Christian* (1969) saw Welch play the part of Priestess of the Whips, commanding a horde of topless rowing slave girls!

Above: Publicity photo from *Bandolero!*, taken on the set built for John Wayne's *The Alamo* in Brackettville, Texas.

Right: On location in Almeria, an area in Spain where many Spaghetti Westerns were shot, for *100 Rifles*.

Opposite: One of the many stunning cheesecake shots taken to promote *Myra Breckinridge*.

ANN-MARGRET

That Ann-Margret would emerge as an internationally acclaimed actress, singer and leading Sixties sex siren would have seemed unthinkable during her early years. The future star was born in Sweden in 1941 and raised in a town near the Arctic Circle, far away from the glamour of Hollywood.

Her birth name is Ann-Margret Olsson. The family moved to the United States in 1946 and she gained citizenship when she was eight years old. Ann-Margret showed early talent for performing while still in school and at Northwestern University she became involved in school performing arts activities, although she never graduated. After leaving the university, she joined a group of aspiring singers called The Suttletones. The group never took off, but her association with them brought Ann-Margret to the attention of comedian George Burns, who featured her on his TV variety programme. Her notices were excellent and she landed a recording contract with RCA. Ann-Margret's albums, often with accompaniment from some of the most prominent names of day, were fairly successful, but not blockbusters. She continued to record into the Seventies, when she had her greatest success with the song 'Love Rush', a hit on the disco charts in 1979.

In 1961, Fox signed her to a multi-year contract. She made her big screen début in Frank Capra's remake of his own film, *Pocketful of Miracles*, with heavyweight stars Bette Davis and Glenn Ford. Ann-Margret had a starring role the following year in the hit musical *State Fair* and gained genuine star status in 1963 as the female lead in *Bye Bye Birdie*. Another smash hit followed in 1964 when she played oppostie Elvis Presley in *Viva Las Vegas*, regarded by many as Presley's best film of the decade. She would be romantically linked with Presley, providing much fodder for the tabloids.

With her bright red hair, perfect body and ability to play wholesome girls while dancing highly suggestively, Ann-Margret fulfilled the fantasies of males of all ages. She also proved she could perform as a dramatic actress, in films such as *Kitten With a Whip* (1964), *The Pleasure Seekers* (1964), *Bus Riley's Back in Town* (1965), *The Cincinnati Kid* (1965) opposite Steve McQueen and *The Swinger* (1966). Less successful was a starring role in Fox's 1966 remake of John Ford's *Stagecoach*. Like so many of her contemporaries, Ann-Margret also capitalised on the Sixties spy movie craze by co-starring with Dean Martin in the Matt Helm hit *Murderers' Row* (1966).

Ann-Margret married actor Roger Smith in 1967 and the couple have been together ever since. During the 1970s her stage career prospered and she performed to sell-out crowds in Las Vegas. In motion pictures, she scored Oscar nominations for Mike Nichols' *Carnal Knowledge* (1971) and Ken Russell's 1975 film adaptation of The Who's *Tommy* (1975). Ann-Margret's career as a performer almost came to an end in 1972 when she tumbled from a stage and suffered severe injuries, which required adherence to a liquid diet for ten weeks. Recovering, she went on to star with John Wayne and Rod Taylor in *The Train Robbers* (1973). She also had a box-office hit in Richard Attenborough's 1978 suspense thriller *Magic*, which co-starred Anthony Hopkins.

Ann-Margret worked consistently through the 1980s, on stage and on TV, earning Golden Globe and Emmy nominations for her guest spots on hit series and in made-for-television movies. In the 1990s, she co-starred with Walter Matthau and Jack Lemmon in the hit comedies *Grumpy Old Men* (1993) and its sequel *Grumpier Old Men* (1995), which also afforded her the opportunity to work with Sophia Loren. In 1994, she published her autobiography, *Ann-Margret: My Story*. Still in-demand in every medium, Ann-Margret won an Emmy for her 2010 guest appearance on *CSI: SVU*.

Opposite top, opposite below and above: Ann-Margret on the set of *The Swinger*. The actress was at her 'sex kitten' peak during the mid-Sixties and this adult sex comedy provided the perfect vehicle for her talents.
Top: Heading way out West – and way out front! – Ann-Margret added some much-needed glamour to the not-so-funny comedy Western *The Villain* (1979, aka *Cactus Jack*).
Left: A rather unsubtle come-hither publicity pose of Ann-Margret on the set of *The Pleasure Seekers*, in which three women go in search of love in Madrid. A kind of precursor to *Sex in the City* – but without the sex!

CARROLL BAKER

Unlike most aspiring actresses, Carroll Baker found fame almost as soon as she entered the film industry. Her first major role was in the highly controversial *Baby Doll*. The shocking image of Baker curled up in bed, provocatively sucking her thumb, caused an outrage, led to demands for the film to be banned and sealed her stardom.

Born in Johnstown, Pennsylvania in 1931, Baker gravitated to New York City in the early 1950s and enrolled at the prestigious Actors Studio. Her first credited film role was in the 1953 Esther Williams movie *Easy to Love* and while at the Actors Studio she impressed the legendary Elia Kazan, who cast her in his 1956 picture *Baby Doll* as the teenage bride of middle-aged Karl Malden. The result was a major hit, earning Baker an Oscar nomination for Best Supporting Actress. However, *Baby Doll* was not Baker's only major film in 1956. Immediately prior to the film's release, she was seen in a key role in George Stevens' blockbuster *Giant*. Just a short period in to her career, Baker was sharing the screen with Rock Hudson, Elizabeth Taylor and James Dean.

Baker's star continued to rise through to the mid-Sixties. She had a leading role in William Wyler's epic 1958 Western *The Big Country*, co-starring with Gregory Peck, Charlton Heston and Jean Simmons. Other major films of this period include *The Miracle* (1959) with Roger Moore, *Bridge to the Sun* (1961), *Something Wild* (1961, another film that elicited controversy due to its sexual content) and *Station Six Sahara* (1962), in which Baker's character caused tension and jealousy as the only female among a group of men living in the desert. She had an important role in MGM's

blockbuster 1962 Cinerama production, *How the West Was Won,* which became one of the highest grossing films of all time. Her career and box-office drawing power peaked in 1964 with the film adaptation of Harold Robbins' bestseller *The Carpetbaggers*. Critics called it an all-star, upscale dirty movie, but audiences loved it and *The Carpetbaggers* was the highest grossing film of the year. That same year she took the female lead in *Cheyenne Autumn* (1964), the last Western directed by John Ford.

Following these successive hits, Baker made some high-profile but ill-advised movies for producer Joseph E. Levine and Paramount Pictures. *Sylvia* (1965) cast her as the would-be bride of a millionaire who discovers shocking secrets about her past. The movie bombed with critics and public alike. Her next film, *Harlow* (1965), was a Levine production that featured Baker as the ill-fated screen legend Jean Harlow. The movie received a big build-up, but negative reviews ensured that it, too, failed. (Carol Lynley starred in another film, also titled *Harlow*, that same year, which hardly helped matters.) Baker wanted to withdraw from making any more films for Levine or Paramount Pictures, resulting in legal battles and the actress souring on Hollywood.

She consequently moved to Europe in the late 1960s and appeared almost exclusively in movies rarely seen by English-speaking audiences, although some have built a dedicated following over the years. Amongst the more familiar titles for cult cinema fans are *The Sweet Body of Deborah* (1967),

So Sweet... So Perverse* (1969) and fan-favourite *Baba Yaga* (1973).

Andy Warhol lured Baker back to America to appear in his 1977 film *Andy Warhol's Bad*. Baker then re-entered mainstream cinema, this time as a character actress, her box-office power having diminished in her absence. Still, she found she was a welcome presence in supporting roles in major films like *Star 80* (1983) and *Ironweed* (1987). She also played against type as a villainess in the 1990 Arnold Schwarzenegger comedy *Kindergarten Cop*. Since then, Baker has worked only fleetingly – largely television guest spots – and prefers to stay in self-imposed semi-retirement. She had been married twice before finding her true love, Donald Burton, who she wed in 1978. The couple remained together until Burton's death in 2007. Baker nowadays keeps a low public profile, but does participate in occasional documentaries about the making of her more memorable films.

Top: *Harlow.*
Above: The look of innocence lost? Carroll Baker played the role of Baby Doll Meighan, a 19-year-old virgin who, although married, was not allowed to consummate the union until her 20th birthday, in Elia Kazan's *Baby Doll.*
Left: The unexpected arrival of Carroll Baker at a remote oil pipeline station in the desert drives the five bored men working there to jealousy and violence in their lust for her. The striking art for *Station Six Sahara*, seen here in a trade ad, was by famed film poster artist Tom Chantrell.
Opposite: Baker's role as movie star Rina Marlowe, supposedly based on Jean Harlow in Howard Hughes' *Hell's Angels* (1930), was a major part in the big screen adaptation of Harold Robbins' *The Carpetbaggers.*

Above top: Need we say more? Uschi Digart displaying her ample assets that have made her an enduring cult figure among cinematic sex sirens.

Above centre: Lorna Maitland was her name, and *Lorna* was the title of the film. It was Russ Meyer's first film shot on 35mm, and the first of three he made with the busty beauty.

Above: Angel Ray and Ian Sander in *Beyond the Valley of the Dolls*.

Opposite top: *The Immoral Mr Teas*.

Opposite centre: Japanese poster from *Beyond the Valley of the Dolls*, which was not a sequel to the original *Valley of the Dolls* from 1967. Russ Meyer co-wrote the screenplay with legendary film critic Roger Ebert!

THE RUSS MEYER LADIES

Whilst _Cinema Sex Sirens_ is primarily dedicated to women who were famous for their acting ability as well as their beauty, many others were also considered sex sirens yet were not known for their acting skills. These performers are epitomised by those well-endowed women who appeared in the films of Russ Meyer.

Russ Meyer was an independent producer/director who not only introduced nudity to American audiences, but also became famous and wealthy in the process. In fact, he was so obsessed with large-breasted women that he earned the moniker 'King Leer'. Meyer was an independent producer/director who not only introduced nudity to American audiences, but also became famous and wealthy in the process. He began in 1959 with the comedy _The Immoral Mr Teas_, the story of a man who, under the influence of anaesthetic, appears to see all women completely nude. Of course, this was just an excuse to show naked flesh, but it created quite a scandal upon release. Its success helped launch the 'nudie-cutie' craze. By the mid-Sixties, Meyer had also introduced elements of violence to the mix.

In Meyer's films, women were not simply relegated to being "all breast and no brain" and sometimes the female characters were portrayed as take-charge, liberated women. Still, no one would ever classify Meyer as anything other than a man who happily exploited women's physical assets. Titles such as _Faster, Pussycat! Kill! Kill!_ (1965), _Mondo Topless_ (1966), _Motor Psycho_ (1965) and _Vixen_ (1968), all huge money-makers for Meyer, starred a roster of top-heavy actresses whose breasts became the central theme in the marketing campaigns. Although none of these stars ever seemed poised to become the next Katharine Hepburn, they did gain cult followings that persist even today.

Tura Satana was born in Japan in 1938 and emmigrated to the United States with her family. When the Second World War broke out, the American government ordered anyone of Japanese descent into internment camps for the war's duration, including Satana and her family, who were interred at a camp in Lone Pine, California. Her breasts developed at an early age, and as a teenager she led a turbulent life. She was married at age 13 and became a gang leader for a period of time. Shortly thereafter, she capitalised on her natural assets and became an exotic dancer, working with then-famous strippers like Tempest Storm and Candy Barr. Roles in TV shows such as _The Man from U.N.C.L.E._ and _Burke's Law_ followed.

It was in part her knowledge of martial arts (which it is rumoured she learned due to being raped aged nine) that got her the role of the aggressive Varla in Meyer's _Faster, Pussycat! Kill! Kill!_ in 1965. Director John Waters calls the film "the greatest movie that will ever be made". The closest Satana came to starring in a mainstream Hollywood film was through uncredited cameos in _Irma La Douce_ (1963)

and _Our Man Flint_ (1966). It has been reported that she once dated Elvis Presley and rejected his marriage proposal.

In the 1970s, she appeared in other cult exploitation films, such as Ted V. Mikels' _The Doll Squad_ (1973). She ultimately drifted out of show business to concentrate on the medical profession, working for years in a hospital. However, personal drama continued to stalk her. Satana was once shot by an ex-lover and also spent two years recovering from a broken back in the aftermath of a car crash. She ultimately found happiness through her 1981

marriage to a police officer, a union that lasted until his death in 2000. Perhaps the most bizarre aspect of Satana's career was the fact that silent film legend Harold Lloyd was one of her early mentors. He had befriended her as a teenager and encouraged her to take up acting as a profession. She passed away in 2011 aged 72.

Lorna Maitland was born in 1943 with the name Babara Popejoy and appeared in three of Meyer's films: _Lorna_ (1965), _Mudhoney_ (1965) and _Mondo Topless_ (1966). Maitland had begun her career in entertainment as a dancer in Las Vegas. She got the job in _Lorna_, which Meyer named after her, upon answering an advert in _Daily Variety_. However, she was selected on the strength of her 42-inch bust, which was then very full since she was in the early stages of pregnancy. After working with Meyer again on _Mudhoney_, the two fell out when the director suggested that the film's disappointing box-office take was due to Maitland's breast size having been reduced after she gave birth. Apart from a small role in another non-Meyer movie, Maitland left the world of show business and has since disappeared into obscurity.

Haji, who appeared in _Faster, Pussycat! Kill!_, _Motor Psycho_, _Beyond the Valley of the Dolls_ (1970) and _Supervixens_ (1975), was born Barbarella Catton in Canada in 1946 and worked as a stripper before being cast by Meyer. Author Steve Sullivan included her in his top 1,000 glamorous ladies of the 20th century in his book _Glamorous Girls of the Century_. Today she lives in Malibu, California, refers to her early work as "an exotic actress" and continues to act periodically in cult movies.

Uschi Digard was one of the most famous big-bust models of the Sixties and Seventies. Although born in North Dakota, Digard grew up in Scandinavia during the late Forties. Her bust was an amazing 40DD by the age of 15. After initially appearing in a few soft porn films in her native Sweden, Digard moved to America in 1966 and entered the world of X-rated films. Her first film for Meyer was _Cherry, Harry & Raquel_ in 1970, followed by _The Seven Minutes_ (1971), _Supervixens_ and _Beneath the Valley of the Ultravixens_ (1975). She also appeared in the cult classic _Truck Stop Women_ (1974, with Claudia Jennings), two of the _Ilsa: She Wolf of the S.S._ movies starring Dyanne Thorne and had roles in several mainstream films such as _Kentucky Fried Movie_ (1977), although the parts generally required her to be naked. Now retired, Digard, who can speak eight languages, divides her time between her homes in Palm Springs and Hollywood.

ANGIE DICKINSON

Angie Dickinson, born in 1931 in North Dakota, showed she had brains as well as beauty at an early age. Her father, the publisher of a small newspaper, moved the family to California, close to the heart of Hollywood. Her next step seemed inevitable...

However, first she graduated from high school at only 15 years old and then went on to earn a degree in business. Like so many of her contemporaries, it was her entrance in a beauty contest that whetted her appetite for the spotlight. After she married, she decided to pursue a career in acting. Dickinson didn't experience the hard climb to the top that many actresses faced, but led a charmed life from day one. She landed guest spots on NBC TV variety programmes during the 'golden age' of the new medium, and by the mid-Fifties had progressed to acting roles in some of the era's top dramatic shows. She also began playing small roles in B movies, gaining particularly good notices for director Samuel Fuller's 1957 film *China Gate*.

Dickinson's first major big-screen break came when she was hired by director Howard Hawks to play the female lead in his classic 1959 Western *Rio Bravo*, where she more than held

her own against heavyweights John Wayne and Dean Martin. The following year, Dickinson distinguished herself once again as the leading lady in another testosterone-fuelled romp, the Rat Pack opus *Ocean's Eleven*. She became a close friend (and some say lover of) Frank Sinatra. The floodgates opened and Dickinson was soon co-starring with top leading men like Richard Burton, Roger Moore, Rock Hudson, Burt Reynolds, Kirk Douglas, Gregory Peck, Dick Van Dyke, James Garner and Robert Mitchum. Her films included *Captain Newman, M.D.* (1963), *The Art of Love* (1965), *Cast a Giant Shadow* (1966), *The Chase* (1966) and, one of her most important movies, John Boorman's 1967 crime classic *Point Blank*, in which she starred with Lee Marvin. She was also the female lead in director Don Siegel's 1964 film, *The Killers*, again with Lee Marvin. The movie was shot for TV but was deemed too

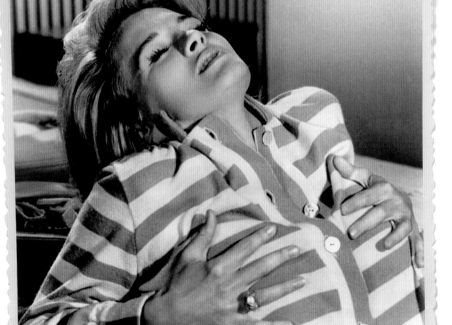

violent and was consequently released in cinemas. The film afforded Dickinson the distinction of co-starring with Ronald Reagan in his last acting appearance prior to entering the political arena. In the 1970s, she starred in Roger Vadim's *Pretty Maids All in a Row* (1971) and also won many new fans with her long-running TV series *Police Woman*, which earned her a Golden Globe award and Emmy and BAFTA nominations. And in 1974 she scored a major cult-film hit in the title role of *Big Bad Mama*.

Dickinson' life has not been all glamour. She married composer Burt Bacharach in the mid-Sixties, but their daughter Nikki, who was born in 1966, suffered from numerous serious health problems. For years, Dickinson's acting career played second fiddle to caring for her daughter. Tragically, in 2007, Nikki committed suicide. Dickinson continues to act today when she receives a script she finds intriguing enough. Her remarkably enduring career led her to be named by *Playboy* as one of the '100 Sexiest Stars of the Century'.

Top: *Rio Bravo*.
Left: Dickinson's sexual presence in John Boorman's *Point Blank* was electrifying.

JANE FONDA

Virtually every baby boomer is familiar with the long career of Jane Fonda, but most probably don't know that she was born with the name Lady Jayne Seymour Fonda (named after a wife of King Henry VIII). The daughter of acting legend Henry Fonda, Jane had show business in her blood.

Her brother Peter also followed in their father's footsteps, as has Peter's daughter Bridget Fonda. Thus the Fondas can make claim to being a legitimate acting dynasty.

Despite her background of financial privilege, Jane Fonda's life has been tumultuous. Her mother committed suicide when she was 12 years old and her father was a rather remote and unemotional figure, more concerned with his career than with raising children. He remarried, but that union ended in divorce, adding more emotional turmoil to Jane's life. As a teenager, Fonda dabbled in acting, appearing in a stage production with her father. She later attended Vassar College, but became enamoured of acting as a profession. She terminated her formal education to study at the legendary Actors Studio in New York, where she was taught by Lee Strasberg.

Fonda starred in Broadway shows before making her film début in the comedy *Tall Story* (1960), recreating a role she had played on stage. She starred in *The Chapman Report* (1962), based a novel inspired by Kinsey's famous sex report, and appeared opposite Rod Taylor and Cliff Robertson in the 1963 comedy *Sunday in New York,* which pushed the envelope with its story about a sexually charged young woman trying to fend off several suitors intent on relieving her of her virginity. It was with the Western comedy *Cat Ballou* (1965), however, that Fonda became a major box-office star. The film may have won Lee Marvin the Oscar, but Fonda's career also benefited greatly. She appeared in director Arthur Penn's star-packed drama *The Chase* (1966) opposite Marlon Brando and Robert Redford, and then

reteamed with Redford on the box-office smash *Barefoot in the Park* (1967), adapted from Neil Simon's hit play.

In 1965 she married filmmaker Roger Vadim and made several films with him, including the notorious 1968 sci-fi epic *Barbarella*, in which Fonda shed her clothing and cemented her reputation as a sex siren. It was an image she would soon regret as she became more committed to women's liberation. Vadim also directed Jane and her brother, Peter, in the arthouse portmanteau horror film *Spirits of the Dead* (1968).

Top: *Cat Ballou.*
Below: French lobby card depicting the heroine's lesbian encounter in the adult sci-fi comedy *Barbarella*. The film was directed by Fonda's then-husband, Roger Vadim.

As the Vietnam War progressed during the 1960s, Fonda became an outspoken political opponent of American foreign policy. She co-founded an entertainment troupe named FTA [Fuck the Army] which argued that the US government's policy in Vietnam was dishonest and based on the suppression of the indigenous people. Fonda also advocated for Native American rights, the Black Panther movement and the plight of Palestinians, who she felt were oppressed by Israel. Her most controversial act was a visit to North Vietnam in 1972. She was photographed sitting behind a North Vietnamese anti-aircraft gun, an act that shocked the world, earned her the nickname 'Hanoi Jane' and provoked condemnation that has lasted to this day. Fonda also cast doubt on claims that released POWs were actually tortured by their North Vietnamese captors. In 1973, having divorced Vadim, Fonda married political activist Tom Hayden, but that marriage ultimately ended in divorce as well.

None of her controversial stances hurt her film career. She gained an Oscar nomination for the 1969 movie *They Shoot Horses, Don't They?* In 1972, she won the Best Actress Oscar for playing a prostitute in *Klute* (1971). She won another Oscar for her work in *Coming Home* (1978) and was nominated for *Julia* (1977), *The China Syndrome* (1979), *On Golden Pond* (1981, with father Henry Fonda) and *The Morning After* (1986).

In the 1980s Fonda introduced a series of exercise videos and books that became international sensations. The seemingly ageless star is still putting out 'sequels' today. She retired from acting for many years and married CNN founder and tycoon Ted Turner, but this marriage ultimately failed as well. Fonda claims she has found religion and has embraced Christianity in recent years. She continues to be an activist, serving as a goodwill ambassador for the United Nations and championing women's rights.

Fonda returned to the screen in 2005 after a 14-year self-imposed retirement, but her fans were perplexed due to her choice of rather undistinguished movies. That same year she authored her autobiography and tried to explain her controversial past. At various times she has seemingly apologised for some of her comments and actions during the Vietnam War era, while on other occasions she's remained unrepentant.

Jane Fonda's destiny seems assured: she will be adored by social liberals and loathed by conservatives, but few would deny her position as one of the most enduring and important actresses of her era.

Above left and top right: Barbarella may have been sent to save the Earth, but she couldn't save the box office. The film was a major flop when released in 1968, despite a provocative and expensive advertising campaign.

Above right: Probably her best-remembered role of the Seventies, Jane Fonda's performance as the prostitute Bree Daniels in *Klute* won her the Academy Award for Best Actress in 1972.

Left: *Spirits of the Dead*, a three-story omnibus based on tales by Edgar Allan Poe, featured Fonda in 'Metzengerstein', the tale of a Countess who murders a man who rejects her romantic overtures.

JANET LEIGH

Janet Leigh owed her start to Norma Shearer, who happened upon her photograph and passed it on to talent agent Lew Wasserman. Wasserman recognised Leigh's extraordinary beauty, signed her as a client and secured a contract with MGM, despite Leigh's complete lack of acting experience! And so a legendary Hollywood career was born.

Leigh, whose birth name was Jeanette Helen Morrison, was born in California in 1927. She made her screen début in *The Romance of Rosy Ridge* in 1947. The film may have been a forgettable trifle, but Leigh commanded a major role, starring opposite Van Johnson. Within a year, Leigh was considered one of Hollywood's most promising rising stars.

MGM was quick to cast their new star in a variety of roles, mostly in crowd-pleasers like *If Winter Comes* (1947), the Lassie adventure *Hills of Home* (1948), the all-star musical *Words and Music* (1948), *Little Women* (1949) and *Angels in the Outfield* (1951). By 1948, Leigh had already been married twice. She first married at age 16, although the union was annulled the same year, and her second marriage lasted just two years before ending in divorce. By 1949, Leigh had begun dating future matinee idol Tony Curtis. The couple married in 1951 and stayed together until 1962, when they divorced. Leigh and Curtis had two daughters, Jamie Lee and Kelly, both of whom entered the acting profession.

After starring with Stewart Granger in *Scaramouche* (1952) and James Stewart in *The Naked Spur* (1953), Leigh and Tony Curtis co-starred in *Houdini* (1953), *The Black Shield of Falworth* (1954) and the major box-office hit *The Vikings* (1958). She also appeared with Dean Martin and Jerry Lewis in *Living It Up* (1954), as well as Howard Hughes' notorious *Jet Pilot*, a sexed up Cold War adventure with John Wayne which had been filmed in 1949 but was not released until 1957. Towards the end of the decade she also starred in Orson Welles' *A Touch of Evil* opposite Charlton Heston. Considered a classic today, it actually found little success at the American box office on its initial release in 1958.

In 1960, Leigh was cast in her most famous role, as Marion Crane, the ill-fated young woman who is murdered at the Bates Motel in Alfred Hitchcock's *Psycho*. Hitchcock wanted a major star for the role since he correctly believed audiences would be stunned when she was killed off early in the picture. He also took advantage of her more than ample bust size and used every opportunity he could to feature the actress in her lingerie to titillate the audience. In fact, the marketing people used images of Leigh

in her bra in the film's publicity as a draw too. For her performance, Leigh won the Golden Globe Award and was nominated for a Best Supporting Actress Oscar.

Leigh appeared in other major box-office hits in the early Sixties, including John Frankenheimer's classic thriller *The Manchurian Candidate* (1962), the popular musical *Bye Bye Birdie* (1963) and the comedy *Wives and Lovers* (1963), which reunited her with Van Johnson.

By the mid-Sixties, however, her box-office power was waning and she found herself relegated to supporting roles. The quality of the films also varied widely, from the obscure Western *Kid Rodelo* (1966) to the Jerry Lewis comedy *Three on a Couch* (1966) and the critically acclaimed *Harper* (1966, aka *The Moving Target*) starring Paul Newman. Leigh also made a memorable appearance, cast against type as a nymphomaniac killer spy, in a two-part episode of *The Man From U.N.C.L.E.* that became a box-office hit when released theatrically in 1967 as *The Spy in the Green Hat*.

By the 1970s, Leigh's talents were largely under-utilised by the movie studios. She starred in the unintentionally hilarious *Night of the Lepus* (1972), in which she fended off an invasion of giant bunny rabbits, and worked primarily making guest appearances on popular TV programmes. In 1998, she co-starred with her daughter Jamie Lee in the horror film *Halloween H2O: 20 Years Later*, the pair having also acted together almost 20 years earlier in John Carpenter's *The Fog* (1980). She also proved to be a prolific author. Her memoirs, published in 1984 under the title *There Really Was a Hollywood*, became a bestseller. She also wrote two novels and a book about the making of *Psycho*. She had married her fourth husband, stockbroker Robert Brandt, in 1962. They were separated only by her death in 2004.

Left: Leigh in sexy saloon girl attire for the little-seen Western *Kid Rodelo*.
Opposite: Janet Leigh's role in Alfred Hitchcock's *Psycho* may have been short, but the actress made an indelible impression – especially in the scenes where she appeared in her bra! – and won an Oscar nomination as the ill-fated Marion Crane.

JILL ST. JOHN

If it seems that many baby boomers can't remember a time when Jill St. John was not in the film industry, it's because she made her début as a child and the radiant actress was quickly on her way to a career that would encompass James Bond and roles opposite many of the era's most important leading men.

Born in California in 1940 as Jill Arlyn Oppenheim, St. John almost immediately became a popular presence on television and in feature films. She was signed as a contract player by Universal Pictures at the tender age of 16 and her first credited big-screen appearance was in the romance *Summer Love* (1958). More prestigious films followed, such as *The Lost World* (1960), *The Roman Spring of Mrs. Stone* (1961) and *Tender is the Night* (1962), and St. John was nominated for a Golden Globe award for her performance in the hit 1963 comedy *Come Blow Your Horn* opposite Frank Sinatra. That same year, she had the female lead in two other popular comedies: *Who's Minding the Store* with Jerry Lewis and *Who's Been Sleeping in My Bed?* alongside Dean Martin. Thus, St. John starred back-to-back with both members of the famous comedy team after their break-up in the 1950s. She also took part in the mid-Sixties spy movie fad, starring with Rod Taylor in *The Liquidator* (1965). She then had a prominent role in the 1966 all-star bomb *The Oscar*.

In 1967, St. John appeared with future husband Robert Wagner in the detective film *Banning*. That same year, she enjoyed one of her most high-profile roles as a streetwise glamour girl, reuniting with Frank Sinatra in the hit film *Tony Rome*. Curiously, St. John did not make another feature film for four years, when she returned to star as Tiffany Case in the 1971 James Bond film *Diamonds Are Forever,* which marked Sean Connery's return as 007 after a four-year self-imposed absence. The picture was a massive hit, but St. John seemed disinterested in pursuing feature films. She has made only a handful over the ensuing decades, but never faded from public view because her active romantic life provided fodder for the tabloid press.

Today, St. John remains married to her fourth husband, Robert Wagner, whom she wed in 1990. She has never borne children but has three stepdaughters. Professionally, St. John seems to have retired, and has not acted in films or on television since 2002, although she occasionally appears in DVD documentaries about her past films.

Top: Costume test for *Tony Rome*.

DRIVE-IN GALS

Although all the women in this book have willingly embraced their status as sex symbols, the majority consider themselves serious actresses and career professionals. However, as the barriers of censorship continued to crumble, some actresses had no illusions about achieving success through acting ability alone.

They were content to utilise their physical assets to advance their careers in sexually explicit films. These were not pornographic productions, at least by today's standards. Rather, they became known as softcore porn – mildly titillating movies that could be shown at 'respectable' local theatres. A host of such films were produced in England during the Seventies, mainly comedies, and all had one thing in common – an abundance of exposed female flesh. Ultimately, the audience only wanted to see 'tits and bums', and being comedies it seemed socially acceptable for women to view them as well. No longer was on-screen nudity the exclusive realm of a trenchcoat-across-the-lap male audience. Most of the actresses recognised that their popularity might well be fleeting. Nevertheless, some of these ladies achieved a surprising degree of fame. Ex-pornographic model turned actress Mary Millington became particularly well-known in England for such ventures and a few actresses in America and Europe also gained devoted cult followings.

One actress to gain a degree of fame from exploitation films was Claudia Jennings. Born Mary Eileen Chesterton in 1949, she began modeling in her teenage years and, after working as a receptionist for the Playboy organisation, eventually ended up in the pages

of its magazine as a Playmate centerfold in 1969. She was then named Playmate of the Year in 1970. This was also the period when she began acting in sexploitation films – low budget flicks made for the drive-in crowd, who simply demanded a steady diet of violence, car chases and, of course, the frequent viewing of female flesh. Jennings was perfect for the part. Her ample assets compensated for her lack of training as an actress. Jennings' most notable role was in the 1974 film *Gator Bait*, playing a feisty (and always half-dressed) girl living deep in the swamps and fending for her family by engaging in the illicit poaching trade. Other Jennings gems include *Truck Stop Women* (1974), which also starred the titanic Uschi Digard, *Sisters of Death* (1977), Roger Corman's *Deathsport* (1978) and *Fast Company* (1979). Jennings also had very minor parts in major studio fare such as *The Love Machine* (1971), *40 Carats* (1973), *The Man Who Fell to Earth* (1976) and even an episode of *The Brady Bunch*. However, her success was clearly tagged to the sexploitation genre. Tragically, that success was cut short when Jennings died in a car accident, aged just 29.

For those of you who are aware of the 1970s films featuring the wicked Nazi villainess Ilsa, then the actress Dyanne Thorne will be a firm favourite. This stunning-looking woman started her career as a Las Vegas showgirl and posed nude for pin-up magazines in her late teens. The size of her bust (37D) ensured immediate attention among sexploitation film producers. Her first foray into the genre came via Joe Sarno, appearing in his 1964 movie *Sin in the Suburbs*, which was followed by *The Erotic Adventures of Pinocchio* (1971), *Point of Terror* (1971) and *Blood Sabbath* (1972) amongst others.

In 1974, at the age of 42, with a body that would put most women half her age to shame, she took on the role of Ilsa, a cruel Nazi dominatrix, in *Ilsa, She Wolf of the SS*. Soon an enthusiastic cult following started that continues to this day. The titular character was the female commandant of a Nazi concentration camp. Ilsa tortured both male and female inmates alike for her own deviant sexual pleasures. The movie, which was shot on an abandoned set from the old *Hogan's Heroes* TV series, predictably caused an outrage, which of course virtually ensured its success. Using victims of the Holocaust as a tool for sexual titillation was deemed the ultimate taboo. Thorne justified participating in the project, saying: "It was a chance to put my craft to work. Even so, my

Jewish friends were appalled that I would appear in such a film. My husband is Jewish and he went nuts when he first read the script. But as an actress I didn't think about that. I was just playing a role. It was a job to me and I did the best I could with it. I never tried to glorify Ilsa. I felt she was a character to pity, rather than to emulate. I wanted to show the truth about her."

The film, which was banned in Germany, was a huge hit. Despite having been killed at the climax, demand for the character to return was overwhelming. Since commerce trumps logic in the movie industry, Ilsa was resurrected Spock-like for three sequels: *Ilsa, Harem Keeper of the Oil Sheiks* (1976), *Ilsa, the Tigress of Siberia* (1977) and *Ilsa, the Wicked Warden* (1977), the latter directed by Jess Franco and making no attempt to link the character to her Nazi past. Thorne went into self-imposed retirement in 1987 following her appearance as a transsexual father in a mainstream big studio comedy, *Real Men*, opposite James Belushi. Today, Thorne and her husband are ordained ministers and conduct outdoor weddings in Las Vegas. Only in America could you be married by a woman who once played a Nazi commandant and a transsexual parent.

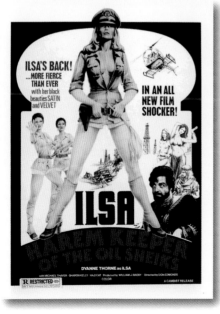

Opposite top: *Ilsa, She Wolf of the SS.*.
Opposite below right: The huntress who became the hunted. Claudia Jennings as Desiree the alligator poacher in *Gator Bait*.
Above: Dyanne Thorne in *Ilsa, Harem Keeper of the Oil Sheiks*.

STELLA STEVENS

One of the top sex symbols to emerge in the Sixties, Stevens career saw her appear opposite Elvis, display expert comic timing with Jerry Lewis and embrace the mid-Sixties spy craze. Hollywood studios also took notice, of both her voluptuous body and her ability to portray the girl next door.

Stella Stevens was born in 1936 as Estelle Caro Eggleston and in 1954, whilst still a teenager, married an electrician called Herman Stephens. They had one child, Andrew Stevens, who later became a successful actor and director in his own right. Though the couple would divorce, Stella adapted her married surname to 'Stevens' when she entered the film business. Stevens made her screen début in 1959 in *Say One for Me*, sharing the Golden Globe for Most Promising Newcomer-Female with future stars Angie Dickinson, Tuesday Weld and Janet Munro. Prominent roles soon followed in *Li'l Abner* (1959) and *Too Late Blues* (1961), opposite Bobby Darin.

Stevens was not shy about capitalising on her natural assets and had three pictorials in *Playboy* during the 1960s. She also had affairs with a number of prominent actors and landed increasingly important film roles as it became clear Stevens could deliver at the box office. In 1962, she co-starred with Elvis Presley in one of his most popular films, *Girls! Girls! Girls!*, although curiously Stevens is reputed to have

balked at appearing in the movie until Paramount inisisted. She also took the female lead in Jerry Lewis' most acclaimed and enduring film, *The Nutty Professor* (1963), and co-starred with Glenn Ford three times over a three year period in *The Courtship of Eddie's Father* (1963), *Advance to the Rear* (1964) and *Rage* (1966).

By the mid-Sixties the spy craze was in full flow and Stevens starred opposite Dean Martin in his first Matt Helm spoof, *The Silencers* (1966), a role that allowed her to display her comedic talents as a bumbling secret agent. She reteamed with Martin in 1968 for the comedy *How to Save a Marriage and Ruin Your Life*. That same year, she acted alongside Rosalind Russell in another comedy, *Where Angels Go… Trouble Follows*. Stevens starred with David McCallum in the underrated thriller *Sol Madrid* (1968) (UK title: *The Heroin Gang*), playing a woman victimised by a drug gang, and the memorable Sam Peckinpah Western *The Ballad of Cable Hogue* (1970), co-starring with Jason Robards. In 1972 she had a prominent role as

Ernest Borgnine's ill-fated wife in producer Irwin Allen's blockbuster production *The Poseidon Adventure*, a film that still generates considerable fan mail today for the actress.

Since *The Poseidon Adventure*, Stevens' talents have been under-utilised on the big screen, and most of her roles have been in B movies. She has tried her hand at directing on a couple of occasions: with the documentary *The American Heroine* (1979) and the little-seen 1989 film *The Ranch*, featuring her son Andrew. Although quality roles in feature films began to evaporate, Stevens found a more receptive welcome on television and has worked consistently in that format for decades. She has also been a popular presence in regional stage productions of famous shows. Today, Stevens indulges in her passion for sports, fitness and horse riding. Her web site at www.stellastevens.com promotes her latest ventures and allows fans to communicate directly with her. In 1999, she also published her first novel, *Razzle Dazzle*, thus earning her a self-described status as 'writer-comedienne-producer-director-actor-star'.

Opposite top: *How to Save a Marriage and Ruin Your Life*.

Opposite below: Stella starred opposite current Man From U.N.C.L.E. favourite David McCallum in *Sol Madrid*.

Above: Being exposed (literally!) as a spy in *The Silencers*. Seen here with Daliah Lavi and Dean Martin, Stella played the sexy but bumbling secret agent Gail Hendricks. The film was a major box office hit in 1966, a year in which no James Bond film was released.

Left: Taking an outdoor bath in Sam Peckinpah's *The Ballad of Cable Hogue*. Stella played Hildy, the tart with a heart, opposite Jason Robards in the titular role of hobo Cable Hogue.

SHARON TATE

A rising female star during the 1960s, Sharon Tate's name has since become synonymous with one of the most infamous crimes in American history. Consequently, her considerable talents as an actress have often been overlooked.

She was born in Texas in 1943 and had an improbable road to stardom. The daughter of an American army officer, Tate and her two sisters were uprooted regularly and relocated every time their father was sent to a new base. It made for a challenging childhood, as they found it difficult to develop long-term friendships. Ironically, it was only when the family moved to Verona, Italy that Tate found her niche. She gained a measure of celebrity as a local beauty and visited the nearby set of the Fox film *Hemingway's Adventures of a Young Man* (1962). She caught the eye of the movie's star, Richard Beymer, and began dating him. Beymer was convinced that Tate had a future in the movie industry and persuaded her to pursue acting, whetting her appetite by arranging for her to have a bit part in the film. Prior to this, she had been determined to study psychiatry.

Tate was now enthused about making movies. She met Jack Palance whilst he was filming *Barabbas* (1961) during this period, and he, too, was impressed. Palance gave her a small role in the movie, but it wasn't until the family moved to Los Angeles in 1962 that Tate made definite steps towards an acting career. Producer Martin Ransohoff signed her to a seven-year contract, but explained that he wanted her to hone her skills as an actress before playing anything but the briefest of roles on popular TV shows. Over the next couple of years, Tate auditioned for major parts in *The Cincinnati Kid* (1965) and *The Sound of Music* (1965), but was judged too inexperienced. Ransohoff acted as her mentor during this time, which led to brief appearances in his films *The Americanization of Emily* (1964) and the Taylor/Burton sudser *The Sandpiper* (1965). Both films were substantial hits and helped to slowly gain Tate the exposure she needed.

Tate finally enjoyed a major, memorable role in Ransohoff's 1966 gothic chiller *Eye of the Devil*, sharing the screen with legends David Niven and Deborah Kerr. She was cast as a beautiful but opaque young woman with an air of mystery and menace about her. Ransohoff was so impressed by her screen presence that he had the film's production featurette focus on his star-in-the-making. It was around this time that Sharon Tate and director Roman Polanski met. He was a young *wunderkind*, a major talent in the new wave of European filmmaking about to branch out into mainstream, big studio films.

Ransohoff was producing his horror movie spoof *The Fearless Vampire Killers* (1967, aka *Dance of the Vampires*) and was dismayed to learn that Polanski intended to cast Jill St. John

as the female lead. He pressured Polanski to give Tate the role. Although Polanski was initially unimpressed with her acting ability, he began to sense that she had an innocence and vulnerability which would work on screen. The two also found that romance was blossoming. When the film was released, Polanski was aghast at the cuts the studio made against his wishes. The movie bombed but has today become a popular cult movie. Similarly, *Eye of the Devil* had also underwhelmed audiences and critics and Tate's status as 'The Next Big Thing' was beginning to look doubtful.

She accepted one of the lead roles in the 1967 version of Jacqueline Susann's novel *Valley of the Dolls*, focusing on the seedy side of Hollywood. The book had been a publishing sensation, but the film version was mocked by critics despite an impressive cast. Nevertheless, on this occasion the reviews meant little, as the pent-up demand for the film ensured it opened to excellent business.

Tate emerged with the lion's share of the publicity and her image graced magazine covers around the world. Her new-found celebrity status helped ease the blow of missing out on the lead role of *Rosemary's Baby* (1968), the movie that would make Polanski a household name in America.

Tate and Polanski married in 1967, becoming the focus of media attention as the film industry's hippest couple. They partied with acting and rock 'n' roll legends and Polanski did little to hide his philandering with other women, although Tate did say that he lied about his affairs and she pretended to believe him. Tate's next major role was as a bumbling but beautiful secret agent in Dean Martin's fourth Matt Helm film, *The Wrecking Crew* (1969). The movie was scorned by critics, but Martin had a built-in audience for the franchise. He intended to film another Helm movie, *The Ravagers*, and told Tate he wanted her to reprise her role. However, tragedy intervened. Tate's final screen appearance was in the little-seen 1969 arthouse movie, *12+1* (aka *The Thirteen Chairs*), in which she starred with Orson Welles.

Opposite: Although a scene in the film, Sarah Shagal (get it?) played by Sharon Tate was not shown naked in *The Fearless Vampire Killers*. However, she did pose for a series of topless and near-naked photographs for the film's publicity and a special *Playboy* spread.

Above: Illya Kuryakin (David McCallum) and a beautiful therapist aid (Tate) race against time to seek a formula that accelerates healing in 'The Girls of Nazarone Affair', a 1965 episode from *The Man From U.N.C.L.E.*

Above right middle: On the backlot of MGM British Studios, Borehamwood, England, during the filming of *The Fearless Vampire Killers*.

Right: Director Roman Polanski took every opportunity to expose his wife's natural assets, as seen here in a scene from *The Fearless Vampire Killers*.

In August 1969, Tate was at home in Los Angeles whilst Polanski was working in Europe. She was only two weeks away from giving birth to their first child and Polanski was due back for the delivery. On the evening of August 8, Tate was entertaining friends in her Benedict Canyon home, including former beau and celebrity hair stylist Jay Sebring. During the course of the night, Tate, Sebring and three other people were gruesomely murdered. The barbarity of the killings shocked the world and placed Hollywood in a state of panic. The murderers were members of a cult led by Charles Manson, a charismatic self-professed Messiah figure, who had also ordered an elderly couple murdered around the same time. The Manson Gang, as they became known, were convicted and sentenced to long prison sentences, with Manson serving life in jail. Polanski was said to be devastated by the deaths and has paid homage to Tate in his work over the years.

Today, Sharon Tate's legacy is inextricably linked to the tragedy. She remains a mainstay of American pop culture, but sadly not only because of her talent, but also because of her fate.

MAMIE VAN DOREN

Mamie Van Doren is one of Hollywood's most enduring sex symbols – despite a career mostly spent in largely forgotten B movies and exploitation films. However, with her shapely figure and prominent bust, Van Doren seemed ready made for the film industry.

She was born Joan Lucille Olander in South Dakota in 1931 and was first married whilst still a teenager, although the union proved tumultuous and short-lived. Van Doren was also engaged for a while to boxing champ Jack Dempsey, but when film roles began to appear the relationship broke up. Earlier, she had won several minor beauty contests in the 1940s and sang for a while with the Ted Fio Rito band. It was Howard Hughes who first discovered her after she won the Miss Palm Springs pageant. They dated for a while and Hughes cast Van Doren in his legendary 1949 turkey *Jet Pilot* with John Wayne and Janet Leigh. However, the eccentric producer toyed with the film's special effects for so long that it wasn't released until 1957.

Van Doren gained national attention when the famed artist Alberto Vargas painted her for the cover of *Esquire* magazine in 1951. She appeared in small roles in nondescript films for RKO before heading to New York City, where she worked in stage productions and song-and-dance numbers. However, a contract from Universal Pictures brough her back to Hollywood. Curiously, her name 'Mamie' was derived from President Eisenhower's wife, as her contract began the day of Eisenhower's inauguration. Despite plans by Universal to turn Van Doren into a major star, lightning did not strike immediately. Her small roles in the studio's productions made little impact, her best part coming as Clark Gable's girlfriend in *Teacher's Pet* (1958). However, when Van Doren starred in low-budget, teenage exploitation films, she developed a loyal following. Among these were *Untamed Youth* (1957) and the box-office hit *High School Confidential!* (1958). Clearly there was an audience for Van Doren in movies that showcased the new music sensation rock 'n' roll, particularly when combined with an emphasis on teen sex. Other Van Doren hits from this era include the 'women in prison' B classics *Girls Town* (1959), *The Private Lives of Adam and Eve* (1960) and *Sex Kittens Go to College* (1960).

Van Doren was locked into B movies at Universal and the studio dropped her contract when it expired. She appeared in many low-budget films during the remainder of the 1960s, as well as expanding her talents by creating a nightclub act and performing in touring productions of hit shows. Two of the most memorable film titles were *The Navy vs. the Night Monsters* (1966) and *Voyage to the Planet of Prehistoric Women* (1968). She was very active in helping American troops serving in Vietnam. Van Doren not only toured for them in entertainment shows, but routinely visited wounded soldiers in veteran's hospitals. She also featured nude in *Playboy* magazine spreads. Van Doren's fame endured long after her film career declined. An expert at self-promotion, she gained considerable publicity from the publication of her 1987 autobiography, *Playing the Field: My Story*, in which she claimed to have had affairs with a virtual 'Who's Who' of Hollywood leading men, including Clark Gable, Steve McQueen, Elvis Presley, Warren Beatty and Johnny Carson.

Today, Van Doren is still actively promoting her image as a Hollywood sex siren. She sells both vintage and recent provocative photos on her web site at www.mamievandoren.com.

Van Doren has also recently recorded an album of country and western songs. At an age when most people have long retired, Mamie Van Doren is still making news and exploring new talents.

Opposite: Smoking and sex. It would never be allowed today! Mamie Van Doren in typical Fifties cheesecake pose for *Girls Town*.
Below: It's pretty obvious that Universal Pictures' marketing executives had only one (or perhaps two?) things on their mind when promoting their teen rebellion film *Running Wild* (1955).

NATALiE WOOD

Natalie Wood was born Natalia Nikolaevna Zakharenko in 1938 in California, where her working class parents had settled after fleeing Russia following the Revolution. She entered the industry aged four, grew up on the film sets of Hollywood and became one of the most glamorous stars of the Sixties and Seventies.

'Natasha', as she was affectionately known by her family and younger sister Svetlana, developed an early interest in movies which only increased when the family moved to Los Angeles. Her mother was determined that her daughter would some day be a major star and started her in acting at a very tender age. The strategy worked. 'Natasha' was soon renamed Natalie Wood and became a hot property, landing parts in high-profile Hollywood productions. Her breakthrough role came when, aged nine, she was cast in 20th Century Fox's *Miracle on 34th Street* (1947). The film was an instant holiday classic and young Natalie was soon receiving countless fan letters.

Her lifestyle was glamorous and exciting, but deprived Natalie of anything approaching a normal childhood. Even though she was tutored

for the requisite three hours a day whilst working on major movies, Natalie's playmates were adult actors, directors and crew technicians. Although she worked steadily throughout the early 1950s (including a supporting role in the legendary Biblical turkey *The Silver Chalice* [1954]), Wood didn't catch the attention of the critics and public again in a major way until 1955. The film responsible was *Rebel Without a Cause*, directed by the acclaimed Nicholas Ray and co-starring another legend-in-the-making, James Dean.

Wood almost did not get the role, failing to impress Ray sufficiently with her screen test. However, when she was injured a short time later in a car crash, Ray visited her in hospital and overheard a doctor referring to her as "a juvenile delinquent". Wood joked that if a doctor

believed she was a delinquent then she would be the perfect choice to play a bad girl on-screen. The ploy worked and Wood scored a Best Supporting Actress Oscar nomination for the film. She enjoyed another major success the following year when she appeared opposite John Wayne in John Ford's classic Western *The Searchers*.

Opposite: Wood received critical acclaim for her portrayal of stripper Gypsy Rose Lee in *Gypsy*.

While still a teenager, Wood became the 'it' girl among Hollywood's bachelor set. She dated aspiring young actor Robert Vaughn, and played a crucial role in his early successes. However, it was with Robert Wagner that the sparks really flew and the couple married in 1957. The fact that the marriage lasted only five years encapsulates Wood's fragmented and often erratic love life. Her career was still thriving, however, with leading roles in the hit films *Splendor in the Grass* (Best Actress Oscar nomination) and *West Side Story* (Oscar winner for Best Picture), both released in 1961. This was followed by another major success the next year with *Gypsy*, the biopic of stripper Gypsy Rose Lee. During this period, Wood dated numerous major stars, including Warren Beatty and Elvis Presley. She also continued to be astute about her film roles, gaining another Best Actress Oscar nomination opposite Steve McQueen in the 1963 romance *Love With the Proper Stranger*.

By the mid-Sixties, Wood had proved she could also play light comedy in such films as *Sex and the Single Girl* (1964) and *The Great Race* (1965), although there were occasional

misfires like *Inside Daisy Clover* (1965) and *Penelope* (1966). After the latter film's poor reception, she went into a self-imposed retirement for three years. When she re-emerged, Wood found her audience had not deserted her. Her comeback vehicle was the acclaimed box-office hit *Bob & Carol & Ted & Alice* (1969) co-starring Robert Culp, Dyan Cannon and Elliott Gould in an edgy spoof of modern sexual fantasies among suburban couples.

Wood remarried the same year, this time to producer Richard Gregson. Although the couple had a daughter, Natasha, Wood filed for divorce in 1972, suspecting her husband of infidelity. Wood remarried again that same year when her romance with ex-husband Robert Wagner was reignited. The couple remarried and had a daughter, Courtney. By this time, Wood's sister, now known as Lana Wood, had also enjoyed some success as an actress, most memorably as Plenty O'Toole in the 1971 James Bond film *Diamonds Are Forever*.

As Wood finally achieved personal happiness through her second marriage to Wagner, she seemed to lose interest in acting and her

appearances became more infrequent. She made only two more major films in the ensuing years: the abysmal 1979 all-star disaster film *Meteor*, that itself was a disaster, and the forgettable comedy *The Last Married Couple in America* (1980), although she was still seen frequently on television.

Wood was working on the MGM science fiction thriller *Brainstorm* in 1981 and had almost completed her final scenes when she and Wagner invited her co-star Christopher Walken for a night out on their yacht near Catalina Island.

The evening was to have a tragic ending. Sometime in the night, Wood disappeared from the boat. The trio had been drinking heavily and neither Wagner nor Walken realised she had been missing. Her body was found the next day, clad in her nightgown. The coroner reported that death was due to accidental drowning, although some sceptics remain convinced that there is more to the story.

With her tragic death, Natalie Wood entered the pantheon of Hollywood screen legends who died too young. Her work is still appreciated by legions of movie fans, young and old, today.

Far left: Striking publicity shot for *Gypsy*.
Left: Wood in the ground-breaking sex comedy *Bob & Carol & Ted & Alice*.

BLAXPLOITATION!

Although many sex sirens emerged on screen between the 1940s and 1960s, there is a glaring lack of women of colour who fit into that category. This was primarily due to racial prejudice in Hollywood, where minority actors were generally relegated to minor roles and often shown in a demeaning light.

An exception was Lena Horne, whose superb vocal skills crossed racial boundaries. However, although MGM had her under contract, the studio still insisted upon her sequences being self-contained so they could be easily edited out of prints for theatres in the segregated South. By the 1950s, the surge of the Civil Rights Movement in America made the major studios slowly re-evaluate how they presented minorities. Eventually, stars like Sidney Poitier and Harry Belafonte were given intelligent roles and managed to establish major fan bases. Progress was much slower for black women in the film industry, although by the mid-Sixties there were some dignified characters portrayed on screen. The situation changed even more radically with the advent of blaxploitation films in the early Seventies. Movies like *Shaft* (1971) and *Superfly* (1972) played to the previously neglected black audience, who were eager to patronise pictures they could relate to. In these films, black action heroes kicked The Establishment's ass and it was now white characters who were often relegated to villainous or buffoonish roles. (Some critics have pointed out the irony that these major studio movies were actually funded, produced and distributed by The Establishment, using mostly white writers and directors.)

Following the box-office success of the initial blaxploitation movies, it became clear that new angles were needed to prevent the formula from growing stale. One innovation was to introduce dynamic black female characters, generally with memorable names. Tamara Dobson had a notable success playing the lead in *Cleopatra Jones* (1973). The title character was a sort of female James Bond and Dobson returned to the role in *Cleopatra and the Casino of Gold* two years later. Born in the mid-Forties, Dobson received a degree in fashion illustration before becoming a model, appearing in such celebrated publications as *Vogue*, which brought her to the attention of the film industry – undoubtedly helped by being six-foot two-inches and having a bust measurement of 38 inches. She began her acting career with an un-credited role in *Come Back, Charleston Blue* (1972), followed by *Fuzz* in the same year. In the aftermath of the Cleopatra Jones films, Dobson mainly worked in TV, although she did appear in *Norman... Is That You?* (1976) and *Chained Heat* (1983), starring alongside Linda Blair, Sybil Danning and Stella Stevens in the latter. Dobson eventually retired in the late Eighties and passed away in 2006.

Another memorable female blaxploitation star was Gloria Hendry. Born in 1949 in Florida, but raised in Newark, New Jersey, Hendry's acting career began with a small role in the 1968 Sidney Poitier film *For Love of Ivy*, having been 'spotted' as a 'Bunny' at the Playboy Club. Two small roles in *The Landlord* (1970) and *Across 110th Street* (1972) followed.

However, her main claim to fame was appearing in Roger Moore's first James Bond film, *Live and Let Die* (1973), as villainess Rosie Carver, and thus becoming the first black woman to bed 007. This caused problems when the film was shown in South Africa, where the love scenes were cut due to the country's apartheid policies. Although the Bond directors boldly took on racial prejudice with the casting of Hendry, its shadow still affected the film. In

Ian Fleming's source novel, the lead female character, Solitaire, is black. However, the studio felt the world was not ready for a black female lead. Sadly, their instincts may have been correct; in certain countries, Hendry's image on the film poster was repainted to make her appear white.

Following her Bond role, Hendry made three blaxploitation films in 1973: *Black Caeser* (aka *The Godfather of Harlem*), *Hell Up in Harlem* and *Slaughter's Big Rip-Off*. She co-starred alongside Jim (*Enter the Dragon*) Kelly in *Black Belt Jones* in 1974, and eventually won her first and only lead role that same year in *Savage Sisters*. Today, Hendry is a popular fixture on the fan convention circuit. A talented singer, she currently concentrates on the musical aspects of her career, and has also written her autobiography, *Gloria*, published in 2008.

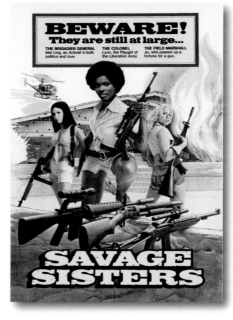

BEWARE!
They are still at large...

THE BRIGADIER GENERAL Mei Ling, an Activist in both politics and love.   THE COLONEL Lynn, the Playgirl of the Liberation Army.   THE FIELD MARSHALL Jo, who passed up a fortune for a gun.

SAVAGE SISTERS

Opposite top: *Coffy*.
Opposite right: Tamara Dobson was promoted as a 'female 007' in the titular role as *Cleopatra Jones*.
Above: Looking drop-dead gorgeous, Tamara Dobson was the object of everyone's desire in *Norman... Is That You?*
Far left: Following her role as a James Bond girl, Gloria Hendry joined Jim Kelly in *Black Belt Jones*, one of the countless martial arts films released in the wake of Bruce Lee's *Enter the Dragon* a year earlier.

The most enduring and successful actress associated with blaxploitation films is undoubtedly Pam Grier. Born in 1949 in North Carolina, Grier's family moved frequently due to her father serving in the US Air Force. She suffered a traumatic event at age six when she was raped by two boys, which she maintains will haunt her for the rest of her life. As a teenager, Grier entered beauty contests, hoping to use the prize money to finance her education. She was working as a secretary at American International Pictures when director Jack Hill recognised her potential. Despite having no formal acting training, he cast her in two of his most successful exploitation films: *The Big Doll House* (1971) and *The Big Bird Cage* (1972). These were not blaxploitation films, but sexploitation movies, capitalising on the seemingly eternal male craving for films about women in prison. (There is now even an acronym for the genre: WIP.)

By the time these films were released, Grier was in prime position to take advantage of the blaxploitation phenomena. She first took the title role in *Coffy* (1973), playing a character described as a 'One Chick Hit Squad'. *Coffy* foreshadowed the *Death Wish* films by presenting a protagonist who tracked down the dregs of society and dispensed her own form of justice. Grier's screen presence earned accolades from influential film critic Roger Ebert, who gushed over her "beautiful face and astonishing form". The film's success meant that Grier was

big box office. She starred in more similarly themed movies, like *Foxy Brown* (1974), *Friday Foster* (1975) and *Sheba, Baby* (1975).

Unlike many other blaxploitation actresses, Grier's career outlasted the genre. She worked steadily in mainstream films like *Greased Lightning* (1977) and *Fort Apache the Bronx* (1981), appearing opposite such Hollywood heavyweights as Richard Pryor and Paul Newman. Grier also had guest slots on top TV series like *Crime Story, The Cosby Show, Miami Vice* and *Night Court*. By the 1990s, her position as a cult figure was assured. A favourite of director Quentin Tarantino, Grier was handed the title role of his 1997 crime opus *Jackie Brown*, and earned a Golden Globe nomination for Best Actress. She appeared in a popular 2004 video by rap artist Snoop Dogg and has recently had a recurring role in the popular TV series *Smallville*. Grier continues to act in major movies.

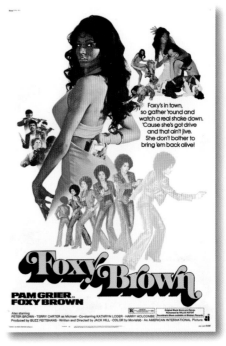

Opposite below: Poster art for *Coffy*, which secured
Pam Grier's status as a blaxploitation icon.
Above left: Don't mess with *Coffy*.
Below left: On the set of *Foxy Brown*.

THE CONTINENTALS

Although Hollywood was rather bold in its depiction of sex during the silent era and in the early days of sound films, the dreaded Hays Code ensured that erotic content in subsequent productions was largely diluted by de facto censorship. However, in Europe different rules clearly applied.

Even as much of the Continent struggled to recover from the ravages of the war, filmmaking entered a bold period that accentuated how drastically Hollywood productions had been compromised by censorship. As a brave new generation of European directors emerged, so, too, did a new generation of sex sirens. And they were not confined by the puritanical shackles of the Hays Code.

Even in the Sixties and Seventies, European productions were still raising more eyebrows than the films that the newly liberated Hollywood studios were offering. *Bob and Carol and Ted and Alice* never did get beyond the talk stage of swinging, but on the Continent

such reticence would have been considered quaint. By the late Sixties and early Seventies, 'scandalous' European imports, such as the notorious *I Am Curious (Yellow)* (1967), the acclaimed *Last Tango in Paris* (1972) and *Emmanuelle* (1974), were 'must-see' events among the urban elite.

With this new wave of European cinema came a generation of female stars (and starlets) whose physical assets were key ingredients in the success of these productions. Whilst some went on to acclaimed careers (Sophia Loren and Claudia Cardinale among them), many never reached that plateau. However, their contributions should nevertheless not be

diminished. Actresses like Monica Vitti, Sybil Danning and Yutte Stensgaard built loyal followings, often on the basis of their appearance in one or two films that have since become cult classics. The European *laissez-faire* attitude towards sex helped ensure these women's images remain ingrained in the minds of movie fans everywhere. Indeed, the Continentals' relatively permissive approach to sex required the lead actresses to have few inhibitions about shedding those bothersome items of clothing and capitalising on their natural beauty. In this section, we pay homage to these memorable sirens of the Continental cinema.

Opposite page: Loosely based on the British comic strip, *Modesty Blaise* featured the sultry-looking Italian actress Monica Vitti in the title role. A parody of the James Bond films, the film was deemed too campy and surrealistic by audiences and proved only a moderate success.

Above left: The sexy Austrian actress Maria Perschy, seen here in a publicity photo from *633 Squadron* (1964), was a frequent female lead in many European films but never quite became a major star.

Top: The strikingly beautiful actress and model Susan Denberg in *An American Dream* (1966).

Above right: Intergalactic sex kitten Sybil Danning in *Battle Beyond the Stars* (1980). The queen of B movies and cheesecake photos, the Austrian actress readily obliged her male followers by posing nude for *Playboy* in 1983.

Left: Although her career was short-lived, Yutte Stensgaard's lesbian scene with Pippa Steel in *Lust for a Vampire* caused a sensation amongst Hammer fans the world over.

URSULA ANDRESS

The scene in *Dr. No* (1962) where Ursula Andress emerges Venus-like from the sea, clad only in a white bikini, has become as iconic as the actress herself. It remains one of the most memorable movie entrances of all time.

Born in Ostermundigen, Bern, Switzerland in 1936, Andress' early life was far removed from the world of show business. Her mother was Swiss and her father was a German diplomat. He somehow fell foul of the Swiss government and was exiled from the country, only to vanish entirely during World War Two. Andress, the third of six children, found a surrogate father in her grandfather, who was a garden designer by profession. In 2002 she would tell *The Guardian*: "My childhood was incredibly unique, almost like the 17th-century. My grandfather was a very strict man and we lived in a big house with a big nursery. I had to work very hard in the greenhouses and cleaning the furnaces out at night – I worked a lot. It taught me respect and discipline, which is such an

enormous lesson. It gave me the strength to confront any obstacle in life."

Like so many other beautiful young women, Andress dreamed of a life beyond the mundane confines of her home town. Her striking beauty not surprisingly led her to show business and she toiled in some minor Italian films before heading for Hollywood. Andress was quickly put under contract by Paramount, although the studio was slow to realise her potential. She was subjected to the usual training rituals for young actresses: classes in etiquette, poise and proper speech. Perhaps because of her heavy accent, the studio decided not to renew her contract – a fact that Andress found emancipating. She became an integral part of an exciting new wave of actors and actresses, all of whom were flirting

with stardom in the 1950s. Andress was romantically linked with Marlon Brando for a time and had a volatile dating relationship with James Dean. One gossip magazine quipped that Dean was learning German so that he and Andress could argue in two languages. Andress began to simultaneously date actor John Derek, and the relationship indirectly saved her life. Due to a date she had with Derek, Andress declined Dean's offer to ride with him on the day of his fatal car crash.

Opposite: Publicity still for *4 For Texas*.
Top: *The Blue Max*.
Below: Ursula with then-boyfriend James Dean at a Hollywood party during the mid-Fifties.

Although both she and Derek were struggling and impoverished young actors, the couple wed in 1957. A taxi driver served as their best man and Andress was allegedly given a ring that didn't fit her finger. The couple's luck improved substantially as Derek began to land prime roles in major films. By contrast, Andress' star did not rise until *Dr. No* producers Albert R. ('Cubby') Broccoli and Harry Saltzman searched the world for the right actress to play Honey Ryder, the beautiful, brave and fiercely independent young woman who became a reluctant ally of James Bond on his first cinematic mission.

In an interview in their book *The Incredible World of 007*, Broccoli told authors Lee Pfeiffer and Philip Lisa how Andress got the part: "We couldn't find a beautiful girl who could act. I went through a lot of rejected photographs and I saw a picture of this beautiful girl with her hair wet – just as [Ian] Fleming had written. Harry said, 'How do you know she can act?' I said, 'The way she looks, she doesn't *have to act*!' I called Max Arnow, who I worked with at Columbia Pictures, who said she talked like a Dutch comic! We were struggling, because in two weeks we were going to shoot the picture. I asked him to make a deal for her and send her

to Jamaica. I told Terence [Young, the director], who said, 'Another disaster!' [Young also originally opposed the casting of Sean Connery as Bond].

Andress' appearance in *Dr. No* was anything but a disaster. Despite her voice being dubbed for the movie, she instantly became a major Sixties glamour girl, her photo gracing newspapers and magazines throughout the world. Although some have disparaged Bond girls as being subservient to men, they are, in fact, generally courageous and independent – qualities epitomised by Andress' portrayal of Honey Ryder.

Unfortunately, Andress' love life was not as successful. She and John Derek divorced in 1966, although they remained friends until his death in 1998. In the immediate aftermath of *Dr. No*, Andress' professional career soared and she was featured in two high-profile pictorials in *Playboy*. On the big screen, she co-starred with Elvis Presley in *Fun in Acapulco* (1963), Frank Sinatra and Dean Martin in *4 for Texas* (1963), and George Peppard in the big-budget First World War epic *The Blue Max* (1966). Andress also appeared amongst the all-star cast of the hit comedy *What's New Pussycat?* (1965). She also achieved iconic status among cult movie fans on

playing the title role in Hammer Films' 1965 remake of *She*, a film Andress professes to loathe, and the Italian science fiction flick *The 10th Victim* (1965). In 1967, she returned to Bondage in the madcap, all-star comedy version of *Casino Royale*, a movie defined by its legendary production problems.

Some major studio films followed, including *The Southern Star* (1969) and *Perfect Friday* (1970), but Andress' box-office power had begun to wane. Throughout the Seventies she bided her time in Italian movies, perhaps most famously with *The Mountain of the Cannibal God* (1978). In 1980, she began a long-term romantic relationship with actor Harry Hamlin, with whom she co-starred in *Clash of the Titans* (1981).

Although the couple eventually separated, the union did produce a son, Dimitri. After his birth, Andress made her role as a mother her primary focus. Consequently, her later screen appearances have been in mostly nondescript films. However, her contribution to screen glamour is inestimable: she was voted as one of the 100 greatest sex symbols of all time by *Empire* magazine and the white bikini from *Dr. No* (which she claims to have sewn herself) sold for £41,125 in 2001.

Top: Although well into her forties, Andress had the physique of a woman half her age when she appeared in *The Mountain of the Cannibal God*.
Above: This still from *The Loves and Times of Scaramouche* (1976) confirms that the actress was still at ease appearing nude in films during the latter part of her career.
Left: The always sexy Andress shared top-billing with Stanley Baker in the crime caper *Perfect Friday*.

BRiGiTTE BARDOT

With the exception of Marilyn Monroe, perhaps no other actress epitomises the cinematic sex symbol more than Brigitte Bardot. Despite almost forty years having passed since she's appeared in a feature film, Bardot's legendary status endures. Indeed, her first name isn't generally used in reference to the iconic actress: the reference to 'Bardot' alone is enough to conjure up images of glamour and eroticism.

Born in Paris in 1933, she initially trained for the ballet and was accepted by the prestigious National Superior Conservatory of Paris for Music and Dance. However, Bardot was soon lured into the more glamorous world of fashion modeling and when her image graced the cover of *Elle* in 1950, film director Roger Vadim was among those impressed. Vadim not only became her mentor, but also her husband. The couple married in 1952 when she turned 18 years old (her mother having forbidden her to marry the previous year).

Under Vadim's influence, Bardot aggressively pursued a career in films, although she did not immediately emerge as a star despite her stunning beauty. Like other aspiring actresses, she laboured in bit parts, making her screen début in the 1952 French farce *Crazy for Love*. Never shy about displaying her assets on celluloid, the uninhibited Bardot became increasingly sought-after. She had top billing in the 1952 French film *The Girl in the Bikini* and played small roles in English-language films like *Act of Love* (1954), *Helen of Troy* (1955) and *Doctor at Sea* (1955).

As her star began to rise, Bardot landed larger roles, although generally in nondescript movies. Vadim, very much at the forefront of the new wave of European filmmakers, was not content with his wife being relegated to such lightweight vehicles. Thus, he decided to embark on a one-man mission to make Bardot an international household name and hit upon a tried-and-true strategy: if you want attention, create controversy. The 1956 French film *...And God Created Woman* cast her as a teenage nymphet who dispenses with clothing as casually as she does her sexual inhibitions. The French being French, the film found an immediate and enthusiastic audience in her native country. However, it was the outrage the movie caused when it opened abroad that cemented its reputation as a *cause*

célèbre. As Vadim predicted, the more the otherwise inconsequential film was debated, the more Bardot was thrust into the international spotlight. Virtually overnight, she became a

household name the world over. However, as so often happens to show business marriages, fame and fortune wreaked havoc on Vadim and Bardot's relationship and they divorced in 1957.

Some of Bardot's French films were distributed by major Hollywood studios. This

was the case with her 1959 hit *Babette Goes to War*, a French-language Second World War comedy that cast her as a bumbling but courageous farm girl who aids British Intelligence in a daring mission behind German lines in occupied France. Columbia Pictures released the movie in America.

Bardot's career may have been thriving, but her love life was the stuff of cinematic melodrama. An intense affair with former *...And God Created Woman* co-star Jean-Louis Trintignant was not hampered by him already being married. It was rumoured to have ended when he was called for national service and Bardot went on to have other affairs. In 1959, she married for the second time, to actor Jacques Charrier. They had a son, Nicolas, who was raised by his father after the couple divorced in 1962. She married German tycoon Gunter Sachs in 1966 but that union was also short-lived, and the couple divorced in 1969. During this period, Bardot also found success as a popular singer throughout Europe. She continued to work regularly in film, though surprisingly never 'went Hollywood', preferring to appear in European productions. An exception was the 1965 comedy *Dear Brigitte*, starring James Stewart as a man whose young son has an unhealthy obsession with Bardot. The legendary actress appeared as herself in the film. That same year, she teamed with fellow French cinematic icon Jeanne Moreau for the Western comedy *Viva Maria!* directed by Louis Malle. Another unusual venture for Bardot was the English-language Western *Shalako* (1968) for producer Euan Lloyd, who was one of the pioneers in selling territorial rights to different distributors around the globe for his big-budget productions. Bardot was cast as Sean Connery's love interest.

Top: *Shalako*.
Above: American one-sheet poster for *Une Parisienne* (1957).

Top: The almost elfin-like Bardot was only 22 when she appeared in this scene in *Mademoiselle Striptease* (1956). The film also starred the then-unknown 19 year-old actress Luciana Paluzzi.

Above: French poster for Roger Vadim's *...And God Created Woman*, the film which exposed Bardot to the world.

Right: Michael Piccolo and Brigitte Bardot played husband and wife in Jean Luc-Godard's *Le Mépris*, a dialogue-heavy arthouse film known internationally as *Contempt*.

Opposite top: Lobby card featuring a sexually suggestive scene in *Come Dance With Me* (1959).

Opposite far right: This stunning image was also used on the French poster for *Le Mépris*.

Despite Bardot's image as the ultimate sex kitten, she was also hired by some of the heavyweights of world cinema during the Sixties. She gave excellent performances in films by Henri-Georges Clouzot (*La Vérité* in 1960), Jean-Luc Godard (*Le Mépris* in 1963, acting alongside Fritz Lang) and, on three occasions, Louis Malle (*A Very Private Affair* in 1962, *Viva Maria!* three years later and finally *Spirits of the Dead* in 1968).

In 1973, Bardot starred in Roger Vadim's film *Don Juan (Or If Don Juan Were a Woman)*, which featured an exotic nude scene where she shared a bed with Jane Birkin. That same year, Bardot shocked the entertainment industry by announcing her retirement from show business. Few believed she could resist the lure of the

spotlight for long, but they were to be proven wrong. Bardot never again stepped before the cameras except to participate in documentaries about subjects and causes she believed in. Like Cary Grant, no amount of money could convince her to resume her cinema career. Bardot lived quietly for years before re-emerging as an animal rights activist in the 1980s when she launched The Brigitte Bardot Foundation for the Welfare and Protection of Animals. Bardot raised millions for the cause, becoming increasingly outspoken and making provocative calls on heads of state to modify government policies to further protect endangered species. She married a fourth time in 1992 to Bernard d'Ormale, an advisor to the National Front, the far right French political party. As of this date,

the marriage remains intact. However, Bardot's advocacy for animal rights grew obsessive and many feel her behaviour has become increasingly eccentric.

Film historians bemoan the screen legend's disinterest in discussing her own past and career, but those characteristics arguably make her a more interesting personality. In an industry in which so many seek the spotlight, Bardot's reticence is seen as refreshing in some quarters. Her unapologetic stand on complex social issues has also won her admiration among many in France's conservative movement, even though liberals have come to loathe her stance. Perhaps it is most fitting that the woman who caused an upheaval in popular culture so many years ago is still 'stirring the pot' today.

Top: The lady needs a hand. Sean Connery is first to offer assistance to the near-naked Brigitte Bardot on the set of *Shalako*.
Above right: Bardot playing guitar in St Tropez during the Sixties.
Right: Brigitte Bardot and Jane Birkin had no qualms about filming their lesbian sequences for Roger Vadim's *Don Juan (Or If Don Juan Were a Woman)*, which was Bardot's final film.
Opposite: *Viva Maria!* How can any woman fail to look good in a basque?

SENTA BERGER

Senta Berger was born in Vienna, Austria in 1941, during the middle of the Second World War. Berger's parents were cultured people – her mother was a teacher and her father a musician – and from an early age she showed off her own musical skills on stage. Soon she was showing those same talents on a world stage...

By 1957, Berger was taking acting lessons at famed schools for the arts. Working in German films, she progressed from minor to supporting roles, and made a brief appearance in her first Hollywood production, *The Journey* (1959). In 1961, she secured her breakthrough role in an English-language film when she was cast in the Cold War thriller *The Secret Ways*. In 2005, the film's producer Euan Lloyd told *Cinema Retro* magazine how she caught his eye. Lloyd said the production had become bogged down trying to find an actress who would be acceptable to both star Richard Widmark and Universal Pictures: "Then, en route to lunch with Dick [Widmark], I spotted *my* vision of the girl we had spent months looking for, right outside Rosenhugl Studios in Vienna, walking causally along the street, swinging her handbag and appearing not to have a trouble in the world... from the rear, a great figure, gorgeous red hair... but what was her face like? I instructed the driver to slow down to let me have a good look at her. What a stunner she was! Absolutely fabulous! I approached her and asked if she was an actress...With a withering 'get lost' look she said, 'Yes, what's it to you?' I explained that Mr Widmark was in the car, would she like to meet him? Expletives in German followed before I could convince her that the star really *was* in the car. She refused to get into the limo, but after meeting Dick on the pavement I persuaded her to join us for lunch. She scored immediately with Widmark and I contracted Senta Berger the next day.

Henceforth, Berger would alternate between Hollywood and European productions and gain a reputation as a skilled actress as well as a head-turner. Berger was cast in the 1963 World War Two drama *The Victors* as part of an all-star cast and also appeared opposite Charlton Heston in director Sam Peckinpah's troubled 1965 film *Major Dundee*. She also began cropping up in high-profile guest spots on American TV, including the part of a femme fatale in a 1964 two-part episode of *The Man From U.N.C.L.E.* which was later re-edited into

the successful feature film *The Spy With My Face* (1966). By the time the movie hit theatres, Berger was a big enough star to figure prominently in the international advertising campaigns.

During the 1960s she became strongly associated with espionage films. In 1966, she took the female lead in *The Quiller Memorandum*, appeared in Euan Lloyd's *The Poppy is Also a Flower* (based on a concept by Ian Fleming, it's the only film to have been produced by the United Nations) and co-starred with Tony Randall in the spy spoof *Our Man in Marrakesh* (aka *Bang ! Bang! You're Dead!*), whilst the following year she was seen in Dean Martin's Matt Helm adventure *The Ambushers*. Berger also had a co-starring role in Kirk Douglas' 1966 production *Cast a Giant Shadow*, which told of the war-torn birth of Israel. In 1969 she appeared in the sexually charged *De Sade* and the following year Berger took the lead role in the cult movie *When Women Had Tails*. One of her last films to receive a major release in English-language territories was Peckinpah's 1977 First World War film *Cross of Iron*.

Berger has worked consistently ever since, winning numerous international film awards as well as expanding her range of talents to singing. Married since 1966 to producer Michael Verhoeven, the couple started their own production company in the Sixties. The mother of two sons (one of whom is the actor Simon Verhoeven), Berger today serves as president of the German Film Academy. In 2006, she published her autobiography, though it may require a sequel, as she is still acting in motion pictures today.

Top: Berger carved a niche playing femme fatales in 1960s spy movies such as the Matt Helm adventure *The Ambushers*.
Left: Senta with Robert Vaughn in *The Spy With My Face*, derived from episodes of *The Man From U.N.C.L.E.* TV series.

CLAUDIA CARDINALE

One of the most legendary and enduring beauties of international cinema, Claudia Cardinale's birth name would have been rather difficult to fit on a cinema marquee: Claude Joséphine Rose Cardinale. But with any name, she clearly had the looks and the talent to be a major star.

She was raised in a household in which Tunisian Arabic and French were the primary languages. As a teenager, she won the title 'The Most Beautiful Italian Girl in Tunisia' and the grand prize – a trip to Venice – was instrumental in changing her plans to become a teacher. The 17-year-old beauty caught the eye of local film producers at the Venice International Film Festival and Cardinale was soon offered an opportunity to study at the Centro Sperimentale di Cinematografia in Rome. Initially reluctant to seize the opportunity, Cardinale and her family ultimately decided to move to Rome so she could pursue an acting career. A contract with Vides Films followed and she made her big

screen début in 1958. Almost immediately, Cardinale fell victim to the temptations of the big city: she became pregnant and gave birth to a boy, Patrizio. The father has never been identified by Cardinale, except to be described as a Frenchman. To avoid a scandal, Cardinale initially identified the baby as her brother. Her life and career were stabilised by producer Franco Cristaldi, who first acted as her mentor and in 1966 became her husband.

Cardinale's career blossomed very quickly. Her stunning looks and perfect figure, along with her charismatic personality, ensured that she found steady work in Italian cinema. Before long she was working with one of Italy's

greatest directors, Luchino Visconti, in the films *Rocco and His Brothers* (1960) and *The Leopard* (1963). However, it was her appearance in Fellini's 1963 masterpiece *8½* that made her an international sensation. Hollywood soon beckoned and Cardinale was given a primary role in the 1964 smash hit comedy *The Pink Panther*, alongside another international beauty, Capucine. That same year, she co-starred with legends John Wayne and Rita Hayworth in Samuel Bronston's big-budget spectacle *Circus World* (aka *The Magnificent Showman*). Despite her ability to speak English, Cardinale was generally dubbed in these productions – a common practice at the time.

Opposite top: *Don't Make Waves.*
Opposite below: Cardinale with Rock Hudson in the thriller *Blindfold.*
Above: Publicity still taken to promote the John Wayne movie, *Circus World.*
Far left: On location in the south of France for the Peter Sellers' comedy *The Pink Panther.*
Left: Maria, the kidnapped wife of a wealthy rancher, was the focal point of director Richard Brooks' Western *The Professionals.* Cardinale's sultry sexuality was perfect casting.

She went on to appear with Rock Hudson in *Blindfold* (1966), Anthony Quinn in *Lost Command* (1966) and Tony Curtis in *Don't Make Waves* (1967). Her two most prominent screen appearances during this era were in director Richard Brooks' classic 1966 western *The Professionals*, with Burt Lancaster and Lee Marvin, and opposite Henry Fonda, Jason Robards and Charles Bronson in Sergio Leone's *Once Upon a Time in the West* (1968).

The latter film was dramatically edited and given a botched American release by Paramount in 1969, but has since been recognised as one of the great Westerns. Despite her success in big studio Hollywood productions, Cardinale preferred to appear in European films, such as *Fitzcarraldo* (1982), and has rarely worked in America since the 1960s. In 1975, she and Franco Cristaldi divorced and she began a relationship with Italian film director Pasquale

Squitieri that continues to this day. The couple have a daughter, also named Claudia.

Although Cardinale, who has lived in Paris in recent years, is secure in her status as one of the screen's eternal beauties, the role she most relishes is Goodwill Ambassador for UNESCO. In this capacity, she devotes much of her time to improving the lives of impoverished women around the world, although she is still tempted to take the occasional film role.

Opposite: *The Professionals.*
Above left and top right: The role of Jill McBain in Sergio Leone's masterpiece *Once Upon Upon a Time in the West* was the pinnacle of Cardinale's career.
Above right: Now in her earlier forties, Cardinale was as sexy as ever playing Eleana, the madam of a Greek brothel, in the Second World War adventure *Escape to Athena* (1979).
Left: 'CC' and 'BB' together in one movie! Belgian poster for comedy Western *The Legend of Frenchie King* (1971).

ANITA EKBERG

Anita Ekberg's striking good looks, charismatic personality and 39-22-36 inch measurements helped her launch a successful modeling career in her teens. It was one that would lead to Hollywood and her iconic performance in Federico Fellini's lauded arthouse hit *La Dolce Vita* (1960).

Born Kerstin Anita Marianne Ekberg in Malmö, Skåne, Sweden in 1931, Anita Ekberg came from a large family. With seven siblings, she strove to find her own identity. Her natural good looks led her to enter beauty contests and Ekberg became a local sensation. She was ultimately awarded the title of Miss Sweden, which enabled her to travel to America to compete in the Miss Universe contest. Soon, Ekberg was signed as a contract player at Universal Studios, despite only having a limited mastery of the English language. As was the custom, Ekberg found herself attending classes to learn poise, athletic ability and acting techniques. Uncertain as to how exploitable Ekberg's talents were, Universal used her as virtual window dressing in minor roles in such diverse films as *The Mississippi Gambler, Abbott and Costello Go to Mars, The Golden Blade* and *Take Me to Town* – all released in 1953. She was generally denied screen credit and, like so many of the era's would-be starlets, seemed destined to fade into oblivion.

Ekberg's unlikely saviour was the legendary John Wayne. Wayne was one of the first major stars to gain independence from the draconian studio system and formed his own production company, Batjac. When casting for his Cold War adventure *Blood Alley* (1955), he signed Ekberg

for a major supporting role as a Chinese girl! She acquitted herself well and won the Golden Globe Award as Most Promising Female Newcomer, which led to more prominent roles. Soon Ekberg was cavorting on-screen with the top box-office attractions of the Fifties, Dean Martin and Jerry Lewis, in the hit films *Artists and Models* (1955) and *Hollywood or Bust* (1956). Next came her most prominent role of the decade, as Helene Kuragina in King Vidor's 1956 epic adaptation of Tolstoy's *War and Peace* opposite Audrey Hepburn and Henry Fonda. Despite these promising opportunities, Ekberg was largely consigned to major roles in B movies like *Screaming Mimi* (1958). Among her early champions was future James Bond producer Albert R. ('Cubby') Broccoli, who was then running Warwick Productions with his partner Irving Allen. Broccoli cast Ekberg as the female lead in the 1956 adventure film *Zarak*, opposite Victor Mature.

In 1960, Ekberg landed the role that would define her career – and assure her standing as a pop culture icon. Federico Fellini cast her in the pivotal role of Sylvia, the elusive seductress who becomes the obsession of Marcelo Mastroianni in the arthouse masterpiece *La Dolce Vita*. Ekberg's cool and aloof demeanour, coupled with her striking physical appearance in a low-

cut black gown, made her a media sensation. The images of Ekberg flirting with Mastroianni in Rome's Trevi Fountain are now truly the stuff of cinematic legend. Fellini would also reunite with her for a segment he directed in the 1962 film *Boccaccio '70*.

Despite these high-profile appearances, major stardom eluded Ekberg, although she did continue to work steadily in nondescript films. In 1963, Cubby Broccoli and his new partner on the James Bond films, Harry Saltzman, cast her opposite Bob Hope in the zany comedy *Call Me Bwana*. Curiously, she also made an impact in a memorable sequence in a film in which she did *not* appear.

In the James Bond movie *From Russia With Love* (1963), Ekberg's face adorns a Turkish billboard for *Call Me Bwana* and a SPECTRE agent is assassinated while escaping on a rope through her 'mouth' down the side of a building! Ekberg has one further connection to the Bond films. Following her divorce from British actor Anthony Steel, to whom she was married from 1956 until 1959, she married actor Rik Van Nutter. Whilst the couple was dining with Broccoli and his wife Dana, Cubby offered the role of CIA agent Felix Leiter to Van Nutter in the 1965 007 blockbuster *Thunderball*.

Although Ekberg was married to Van Nutter between 1963 and 1975, her love life became fodder for the international tabloids. She was rumoured to have had affairs with many high-profile stars, including Frank Sinatra, with whom she co-starred in the 1963 comedy *4 for Texas* alongside Dean Martin and Ursula Andress. Always outspoken and seemingly the epitome of the independent woman, Ekberg was branded a diva. Whilst this made her exploits popular with the international media, she never found another role equal to that of Sylvia in *La Dolce Vita*. Throughout the Sixties, she alternated between European films and Hollywood productions. She was the female lead opposite Tony Randall in the 1965 Hercule Poirot mystery *The Alphabet Murders* and

reunited with Jerry Lewis for the sci-fi comedy *Way… Way Out* (1966), a film criticised on release for its blatant sexual content which was considered inappropriate for Lewis' core family audience. Following an appearance in Vittoria De Sica's 1967 all-star comedy *Woman Times Seven*, Ekberg almost entirely confined her appearances to European films.

Ekberg long ago expressed a desire to have children, but it remained an unfulfilled wish. She seems to have ambiguous feelings about her native Sweden. Published reports say she thinks her talents have never been sufficiently appreciated there, although she does return periodically and has publicly stated that she intends to be buried on Swedish soil. Ekberg has been inactive on the big screen since the late

1990s, but in 2010 returned to Rome to celebrate the 50th anniversary of *La Dolce Vita*. As in decades past, Ekberg was a media sensation and seemed to relish being back in the spotlight. Even after all those years, the lady still knew how to draw a crowd.

Above: Following her move to America, Ekberg soon became a major pin-up. Russ Meyer was often quoted as saying she was the most beautiful woman he had ever photographed and that "her 40D bustline was the most ample in A list Hollywood history"!

Opposite: Ekberg's image as Salma on the original *Zarak* poster was banned in the UK when the House of Lords claimed it was "bordering on the obscene"!
Above left: The embodiment of 'the sweet life' in *La Dolce Vita*. Is that neon sign an anagram?
Above right: Sexploitation doesn't get more blatant than this! United Artists one-sheet for *Valerie* (1957).
Left: One of cinema's great, iconic images. Ekberg at Rome's Trevi Fountain in *La Dolce Vita*.

BRITT EKLAND

Born in Stockholm, Sweden in 1942, Britt Ekland rose to prominence working in England. She's nowadays remembered as much for her relationships with Peter Sellers and Rod Stewart as is she is for her appearances in classics like *Get Carter* and *The Wicker Man*.

Ekland made her screen début as an uncredited extra in Elvis Presley's *G.I. Blues* (1960) and made similar easy-to-miss appearances in films such as *The Prize* (1963) and *Do Not Disturb* (1965). She had a more prominent part in the 1964 American TV movie *A Carol for Another Christmas*, but stardom seemed far from inevitable for the vivacious blonde. Happenstance provided her with an opportunity she could never have dreamed of when her image in an advertisement caught the eye of Peter Sellers. Both were staying at the Dorchester Hotel in London, though Ekland insists her room was more like a 'cupboard'. Sellers invited her for a drink and two weeks later they married.

With Sellers at the height of his career, Ekland found herself on the A list for parties and premieres and co-starred with her husband in *After the Fox* (1966) and *The Bobo* (1967). However, life with Sellers was hardly one of non-stop laughter, as she soon realised he had deep emotional and behavioural problems. The marriage was tumultuous and the couple divorced after four years, a period she called "too long" in a 2010 interview with the BBC. In that same interview, she referred to her marriage as a "difficult life" with a "difficult man".

Ekland was also carving a niche of her own in the film business. In 1967 she co-starred with Yul Brynner in the spy thriller *The Double Man*

and followed that with a breakthrough role as a stripper in the hit 1968 comedy *The Night They Raided Minsky's*, directed by William Friedkin. In 1971, she had the female lead opposite Michael Caine in the British crime classic *Get Carter*, and played the role of Willow in the *The Wicker Man* (1973) with Edward Woodward and Christopher Lee. Now considered a classic, the thriller with supernatural overtones is also fondly remembered for a provocative dance which Ekland's character performs naked. Ironically, a body double was used for much of the scene, as Ekland was pregnant at the time with record producer Lou Adler's child. In between making movies, Ekland's love life was front-page fodder for the Fleet Street tabloids. A high-profile affair with Rod Stewart ended abruptly when she suspected he was cheating on her, which led to a messy palimony suit that was eventually dismissed in court.

In 1974, she scored the most memorable role of her career, starring as bumbling MI6 agent Mary Goodnight in the James Bond film *The Man With the Golden Gun* alongside Roger Moore and Christopher Lee. Ekland badly wanted to be a Bond girl and applied for the role long before a script was completed. She visited the offices of Eon Productions in London, but was being politely dismissed when a chance meeting with Moore seemed to change her luck.

Producer Albert R. ('Cubby') Broccoli called her in to his office months later to inform her she had indeed got the part. The actress was as surprised as she was delighted, and still recalls the film as one of the best experiences of her career.

In the ensuing years, Ekland has appeared in countless films, though most are of B-movie quality (*Casanova & Co* [1977], *Slavers* [1978], and so on). In 1980 she wrote her autobiography, *True Britt*, and later also found success marketing fitness videos. Ekland's still a regular presence on European and British TV, and recently appeared as a contestant on the UK version of *I'm a Celebrity... Get Me Out of Here!* She frequently acts in regional stage productions in England, devotes much of her time to raising awareness of Alzheimer's disease (from which her mother died in 2005) and remains a popular presence at James Bond-related events and autograph fairs around the globe.

Top: *The Wicker Man.*
Below: Britt Ekland as Anna, the wife of a London mobster, having telephone sex with gangster Jack Carter in the cult classic *Get Carter.*
Opposite: Publicity shot from *The Night They Raided Minsky's.* Ekland played an innocent Amish girl who moves to the big city to find work as a dancer and ends up inadvertently inventing striptease when her tops falls off during a dance routine!

GiALLo GiRLS

Like film noir, giallo is another European term, although this time Italian. It is used to describe those crime and mystery films which feature an ample dose of horror and eroticism, and provided memorable parts for a bevy of European beauties.

During the late Sixties and Seventies, Italian cinema came to the fore producing films that were unique, ground-breaking and bizarre in content, often with scenes of explicit sex and violence. It gave the world a trio of famed directors in Dario Argento, Mario Bava and Lucio Fulci, whose films used stylish camerawork and unusual music to produce cult classics. Unlike the mainstream stars mentioned elsewhere in Continental cinema, giallos featured many actresses who didn't achieve real fame, although their iconic status is nevertheless assured.

Probably the best known of the giallo girls is Barbara Bouchet. Born in Germany in 1943, she and her family were settled in an American internment camp following the nation's devastating damage during the Second World War. The family received permission to immigrate to America and settled in California. The natural beauty entered a Miss Gidget contest in San Francisco and emerged the winner, resulting in a three-year stint as a dancer on a local TV show called *The KPIX Dance Party*.

Smitten by this taste of fame, she modeled for magazine covers and appeared in TV commercials. Bouchet initially landed minor roles in all-star comedies like *What a Way to Go!* and *John Goldfarb, Please Come Home*, both released in 1964. She soon earned a more prominent role when director Otto Preminger cast her as Kirk Douglas' floozy wife who is killed on the morning of the Pearl Harbor attack in the Second World War epic *In Harm's Way* (1965). Her drunken shimmying at a navy officer's dance party is still a show-stopper today. Despite the movie's success, Bouchet's found herself in low-budget films, such as the 007-inspired *Agent for H.A.R.M* (1966) and the British spy movie *Danger Route* (1967). She also appeared in a pictorial in the February 1967 issue of *Playboy* before being cast in the 'renegade' James Bond film *Casino Royale* released that same year.

In the 1970s, most of her work came from Europe, especially Italy, where she obtained leading roles in various giallos, crime films and sex comedies such as *The Black Belly of the Tarantula* (1971), *100 Nights of Pleasure* (1972), *The French Sex Murders* (1972), *Caliber 9* (1972) and *Don't Torture a Duckling* (1972). In the 1980s, after making over 80 movies, Bouchet (real name Goutscher) found success on Italian television and formed her own production company to make a series of keep-fit books and videos, as well as opening a fitness studio in Rome. Aged 59, she made an appearance in Martin Scorsese's *Gangs of New York* (2002), which was filmed in Rome, where she still lives and works.

Edwige Fenech delighted European audiences for over a decade by exposing her ample charms in mainly erotic sex comedies that were never released internationally. Although born in French Algeria, Fenech made the majority of her films in Italy. Her giallo credentials were strong, and credits include Mario Bava's *Five Dolls for an August Moon* (1970), two 1972 Sergio Martino films in *Your Vice is a Locked Room and Only I Have the Key* and *All the Colours of the Dark*, *The Case of the Bloody Iris* (1972) and *Strip Nude for Your Killer* (1975).

She also found a strong following in sexploitation films, like *Sex With a Smile* (1976), and this stunning-looking actress has now enjoyed a career spanning 30 years. Today, Fenech has emerged as a successful film producer. Among her credits is the acclaimed 2004 version of *The Merchant of Venice* starring Al Pacino. More recently, she made an appearance in director Eli Roth's 2007 big studio horror film *Hostel: Part II* and was honoured by Quentin Tarantino, who named an American general (played by Mike Myers) Ed Fenech in his Oscar-nominated 2009 film *Inglourious Basterds*.

5 Filles dans une nuit chaude d'Eté

IRA FURSTENBERG · WILLIAM BERGER
EDWIGE FENECH · HOWARD ROSS
HELENA RONEE · TEODORO CORRA
GIUSTINE GALL
EDITH MELONI · MAURO BOSCO
MAURICE POLI
MARIO BAVA   EASTMANCOLOR   P.A.C.

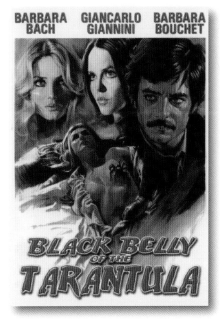

BARBARA BACH   GIANCARLO GIANNINI   BARBARA BOUCHET

BLACK BELLY of the TARANTULA

Opposite top: *In Harm's Way*.
Opposite below: One of the many seductive publicity photos taken of Barbara Bouchet on the set of Otto Preminger's *In Harm's Way*.
Above left: Barbara Bouchet.
Top right: Edwige Fenech.
Above right: Dramatic and eerie French poster for Mario Bava's *Five Dolls for an August Moon*.
Left: Heating up the Cold War! Barbara Bouchet as a communist spy in *Agent for H.A.R.M.*

Above left and left: Crime *does* pay when the crook gets the girl. John Phillip Law and Marisa Mell in Mario Bava's comic-strip actioner, *Danger Diabolik*.
Top right: Ample evidence of why Marisa Mell became a cult figure in Sixties Italian B movies.
Above right: Sultry Rosalba Neri, the Italian bombshell who appeared in countless European erotic films, played one of the women imprisoned on an island in Jess Franco's sleazy *99 Women*.
Opposite: German lobby card for *Slaughter Hotel* (1971), a giallo starring Rosalba Neri, who spends most of her time being threatened by a maniac on the loose in an asylum.

KLAUS KINSKI IN
DER TRIEBMÖRDER
AVIS ASCOT

Austrian-born Marisa Mell is best known for her role as Eva Kant in Mario Bava's cult classic crime thriller *Danger: Diabolik* (1967). Although previously little known in both the UK and USA, she had already appeared in over 20 European films, mostly of German and Italian origin, like *Casanova 70* (1965). Mell also had a sizeable role alongside Cliff Robertson in the British-made spy romp *Masquerade* (1965).

Her stunning beauty had been threatened by a car accident in 1963 that badly disfigured her top lip and nearly resulted in the loss of one eye. After two years undergoing plastic surgery, her recovery was remarkable and, apart from a slight mark on her upper lip, the scarring had disappeared. Mell once turned down a seven-year Hollywood contract, saying the agreement was so restrictive that she would have needed permission to go to the toilet.

During the spy movie craze of the Sixties, Mell starred in a requisite Euro Bond rip-off, this one titled *Secret Agent Super Dragon* (1966) opposite Ray Danton. Mell's fashion model-looks bought her a major pictorial in the March 1968 American edition of *Vogue*, for which she was photographed by the legendary Bert Stern.

The photos were promoting a highly touted stage musical based on the life of Mata Hari, produced by David Merrick and directed by Vincente Minnelli, with Mell starring as the infamous spy alongside Pernell Roberts. Sadly for all concerned, it proved to be one of Merrick's few major misfires and the production was closed down before its New York opening at a loss of $400,000. After the international success of *Danger: Diabolik*, Mell appeared in over 40 movies, including including the giallos *One on Top of the Other* (1969) and *Seven Blood-Stained Orchids* (1972). She died of throat cancer in 1992 aged 53.

Probably the least well known of our quartet is Rosalba Neri. Like many European actresses, Italian-born Neri began her career in the film industry after winning a beauty contest, her first role being in *I pinguini ci guardano* in 1955 at age 15. A year later she was offered a place at the Actors Studio, but turned it down and began her career appearing in comedies and sword-and-sandal productions, including *Esther and the King*, which starred Joan Collins, and Mario Bava's *Hercules in the Haunted World* (1961). In 1961, she was also cast in a small role in

producer Samuel Bronston's blockbuster *El Cid*.

Neri found steady work rather than outright stardom in Eurotrash productions like the 1965 Bond spoof *Two Mafiosi Against Goldfinger* and a number of forgettable spaghetti Westerns. The latter part of the Sixties brought her slightly more prominent roles, particularly *OSS 117 Murder for Sale* (1968), Jess Franco's *99 Women* (1969), which also starred Luciana Paluzzi, and *The Castle of Fu Manchu* (1969), alongside Christopher Lee. Neri headlined *Lady Frankenstein* in 1971, and worked constantly in B movies. Her giallo credits include *Slaughter Hotel* (1971) with Klaus Kinski, *The French Sex Murders* (1972), starring with Barbara Bouchet and Anita Ekberg, and *Smile Before Death* (1972).

Interestingly, she was billed as Sara Bey in some of her films, especially those dubbed and distributed outside of Europe, and has been hacked to death, strangled, shot, decapitated and drowned countless times during her on-screen career. It is thought she retired in 1985, having appeared in almost 100 films.

SYLVA KOSCINA

One of the most successful actresses to came to prominence in the 1960s, primarily through European films, Sylva Koscina was born in Yugoslavia in 1933 of Greek-Polish heritage. Her striking beauty led to a string of interesting roles opposite some of the era's finest leading men.

She emmigrated to Italy as a teenager to live with her sister and her husband. In the 1950s, she attended the University of Naples and began to find success as a model, before moving to Rome. Here Koscina made ends meet between modeling sessions by selling electrical appliances. Her natural good looks led to small roles in Italian films and by the late 1950s she had built a loyal following among European cinemagoers.

In the 1960s, her career blossomed, as did her personal life. She dated (and in 1967 married) film producer Raimondo Castelli and became a popular presence on European TV shows. She proved she had a talent for playing dramatic roles as well as light comedy. Koscina was also open about her sensuality and told British *Photoplay*: "Only on screen do I wear a bra and only when I really have to. Bras are horrible things. I don't need to wear them." Koscina found few male admirers who took issue with her views!

Her star rose dramatically as the female lead opposite Steve Reeves in the 1959 box-office hit *Hercules Unchained*, which spawned a wave of films based on the mythical hero. She also had a cameo in Georges Franju's *Judex* (1963) and a key role in Fellini's 1965 film *Juliet of the Spirits*.

Koscina's career was substantially aided by the James Bond-inspired spy movies of the mid-Sixties. She starred with Dirk Bogarde in the 1964 farce *Hot Enough for June* (aka *Agent 8¾*) and with Horst Buchholz in the hit 1965 espionage film *That Man in Istanbul*. She also made a considerable impact alongside Elke Sommer in the 1967 spy movie *Deadlier Than*

the Male. Attired in outrageously sexy fashions, including skimpy bikinis, the two sex symbols menaced agent Bulldog Drummond, played by Richard Johnson. It was written off upon release as a standard 007 rip-off, but the movie has nevertheless developed a strong cult following over the years.

In 1967 she also co-starred with popular *Man From U.N.C.L.E.* actor David McCallum in the zany comedy *Three Bites of the Apple*. Although it's not a spy movie, the film gave her a bigger international audience by virtue of McCallum's popularity. The following year, Koscina was the female lead opposite two popular male sex symbols of the era: Paul Newman in *The Secret War of Harry Frigg* and Kirk Douglas in *A Lovely Way to Die*. These would be her last big studio Hollywood productions.

Koscina's box-office power began to wane thereafter and she returned to Europe, appearing in cult films like Jess Franco's *Marquis de Sade's Justine* (1969) and the giallos *The Crimes of the Black Cat* (1972) and *So Sweet, So Dead* (1972). She also invested a disproportionate amount of her earnings into financing an ornate villa in Rome, decorating it with expensive artwork and collectibles. This investment resulted in a severe

cash-flow shortage and Koscina faced charges of income tax evasion. She sold her beloved home in 1976 in order to escape her legal troubles.

Although her star had faded outside of European cinema, Koscina found work in many films and on TV until the mid-Nineties. At that time, she was diagnosed with breast cancer amd passed away in 1994 at age 61.

Koscina told *Photoplay* in 1968: "I was determined, when I first attempted to enter the film world, that I would become an actress and nothing else. And that I would make no compromise, and that if I wasn't accepted purely as an actress I would not continue the work. You see, I cannot destroy the woman in me – those are my principles – merely to attain success an actress." By virtue of her legacy, she certainly fulfilled that dream.

Top: *A Lovely Way to Die.*
Left: Saucy scene from *Hot Enough for June.*
Below: Sylva indulges in a little light bondage in the Bulldog Drummond adventure *Deadlier Than the Male.*
Opposite: They had bodies to die for, and that's exactly what happened to the men who crossed their paths. Elke Sommer and Sylva Koscina played a pair of sultry assassins in *Deadlier Than the Male.*

この黄昏はあなた、あゝ私にふれる……全世界の注目をその肌に浴びてエマニエルさらに美しく　さらに大胆に！

続

〈カラー作品〉

シルビア・クリステル
ウンベルト・オルシーニ
カトリーヌ・リヴェ
監督　フレデリック・ラガシュ
音楽　フランシス・レイ
フランス映画／日本ヘラルド映画
オリジナル写真集〈ヘラルド・ブックス刊〉

Emmanuelle II
L'ANTI VIERGE

SYLViA KRiSTEL

Few stars of softcore exploitation films enjoyed the level of success and fame that Sylvia Kristel did in the 1970s and 1980s. Her performance in the ground-breaking *Emmanuelle* ensured she was one of the most instantly recognisable stars of the Seventies.

Born in Utrecht, Holland, Kristel was the daughter of affluent hoteliers. Her home life seemed ideal until she suffered a trauma at age 14 when her father literally ejected her mother and the children from their home after announcing he would be marrying his mistress. This led to her parent's divorce, a devastating emotional event that still haunts her to this day. Largely driven by a desire to show her father that she could succeed without him in her life, Kristel entered a beauty contest in her native Netherlands. She emerged the winner and set out on a path that ultimately led to the motion picture industry.

With her air of innocence and sensuous good looks, Kristel was soon approached about starring in sexploitation films. She was fortunate enough to star in the most successful one of all, the 1974 French movie *Emmanuelle*. Playing a free-spirited young woman, who travels to exotic locations and engages in equally exotic sexual encounters with both men and women, the 22 year-old Kristel became an international star overnight.

Emmanuelle was based on a book by the wife of a French diplomat that purportedly chronicled her own sexual adventures. The fact that the real origins of the book were shrouded in doubt and mystery only enhanced the box office. The film also played in regular theatres, attracting an audience who would never have been seen entering a porn grindhouse, but who now happily lined up to see *Emmanunelle*. Consequently, it became one of the first sexually driven films to appeal to women as much to as it did to men, helped by gorgeous cinematography and lush music that masked the lack of substance behind the routine shedding of clothes.

Kristel was paid only $6,000 for her work on the film, though she did get to spend three months in some of the more exotic areas of Thailand. When the inevitable sequel came about, she received a massive pay increase, earning $150,000. While her professional life prospered, her personal life was turbulent due to a series of marriages and doomed relationships with older men, including a particularly tumultuous long-term affair with British actor Ian McShane.

One positive consequence of these romances was the birth of her son. However, Kristel suffered from other demons besides a broken

heart as she began to use cocaine regularly. The physical effects on her almost resulted in disaster and although she managed to rehabilitate herself, Kristel still retained her passion for drinking and smoking unfiltered cigarettes.

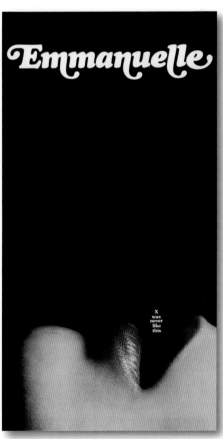

Kristel would go on to star or play cameos in *Emmanunelle* films over a period of years, even when younger actresses were cast for the sex scenes. Like a grand matron, Kristel's association gave each film an air of authenticity during an era when the title was appropriated for numerous unauthorised versions of the franchise. In the late Seventies, she had attempted to branch out into mainstream films by appearing in two major Universal productions. Sadly, they were

both misguided bombs. In *The Concorde – Airport '79*, Kristel has the distinction of appearing in the last of the *Airport* films before the series crash-landed at the end of the disaster movie craze. In the 1980 film *The Nude Bomb*, Kristel was limited to a baffling cameo in a strained feature film based on the classic *Get Smart* TV series.

Kristel found that her broken relationships also drained her of hard-earned money, as she bailed out lovers from their financial debts even as the affairs soured. In 1981, she had a significant hit playing a sexy teacher who seduces a 15 year-old boy in the independent movie *Private Lessons*. Despite a concept that would never receive approval in these more sensitive times, the film was a major success across the globe. Kristel also displayed her charms in both *Lady Chatterley's Lover* (1981) and a sensual screen biography of legendary spy Mata Hari.

However, as the years wore on, her box-office appeal deteriorated. Kristel was philosophical about it all, despite having won and lost a fortune. Today she lives quietly in a modest apartment in Holland and in recent years has written her autobiography. Kristel also successfully fought battles with throat and lung cancer in 2001.

She continues to act periodically and to reflect on a life that included affairs with legends like Roger Vadim, Gerard Depardieu and Warren Beatty. Of her desire to avoid materialism she told *The Telegraph* newspaper in 2007: "I think it's nice to live in an empty place, so you can collect your thoughts. So I've got rid of all clutter. Not necessarily only in my living-room, but in my head."

Opposite: Eroticism gone mainstream: Sylvia Kristal from the original *Emmanuelle* seen on a Japanese poster for *Emmanuelle II*.
Left: American one-sheet poster. The art was toned down for the more puritanical American market.

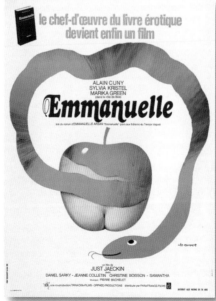

Above and far right: Sylvia Kristel and director Just Jaeckin continued their foray into cinematic eroticism with *Lady Chatterley's Lover*. However, it never gained the notoriety of *Emmanuelle* and was consequently not a major hit.
Opposite: One of the best remembered film stills of all time? The stunningly beautiful Sylvia Kristel will be forever associated with the Emmanuelle character.

GiNA LoLLoBRiGiDA

Gina Lollobrigida's early life mirrored those of a number of other European actresses who rose to fame and fortune in the 1950s and 1960s, as her natural good looks and eye-popping figure ensured a quick passage from local beauty contests to international success.

Born in 1927 in Subiaco, Italy, she lived in a quiet village with her mother, father and three sisters. The family was far removed from the world of show business: her father owned a furniture manufacturing company. Her road to stardom followed a familiar path, with Lollobrigida entering local beauty contests. Although she never emerged a winner, Lollobrigida attracted plenty of attention and before long she was lured into the world of filmmaking. She adopted the stage name Gina, a shortened version of her birth name, Luigina.

She toiled for several years in undistinguished Italian and French films before landing a prominent role in René Clair's 1952 film *Beauties of the Night*. This led to a high-profile part in John Huston's *Beat the Devil* (1954), an off-beat comedy/adventure that gave her the opportunity to co-star with a distinguished cast, notably Humphrey Bogart, Jennifer Jones, Peter Lorre and Robert Morley. Although the film has a cult following today, it was initially regarded as a rare bomb for frequent collaborators Bogart and Huston. Nevertheless, Lollobrigida's career was gaining momentum. She continued to make European productions before heading to Hollywood for another major movie, *Trapeze*

(1956), co-starring with two of the top box-office leads of the day, Burt Lancaster and Tony Curtis. The same year, she also co-starred with Anthony Quinn in a French version of *The Hunchback of Notre Dame*.

In 1959, Lollobrigida's career continued in high gear when she was cast as the female lead in John Sturges' Second World War film *Never So Few*, which featured a powerhouse cast topped by Frank Sinatra and up-and-comers Steve McQueen, Richard Johnson and Charles Bronson. She also starred opposite Yul Brynner in King Vidor's last film, the 'tits and togas' epic *Solomon and Sheba* (1959), which was another significant hit. Lollobrigida's star was rising rapidly and more roles in major studio films followed. In *Go Naked in the World* (1961), she was seen alongside Anthony Franciosa and Ernest Borgnine, but retro-movie lovers primarily remember the production for the provocative series of publicity stills of Lollobrigida dancing suggestively in a tight dress.

One of her biggest hits was also released in 1961, the romantic comedy *Come September*, in which she appeared with Rock Hudson, then at the peak of his career. Her popularity was such

that she received the Golden Globe Award for World Film Favorite. However, this marked the peak of her career. In 1964, Lollobrigida co-starred with Sean Connery and Ralph Richardson in *Woman of Straw*, in which she gave a powerful performance as a woman whose lover frames her for murder. The film remains quite underrated, and was a box-office and critical failure upon release. She reunited with Rock Hudson in 1965 for another lightweight romp, *Strange Bedfellows*, and teamed with Alec Guinness in the 1966 madcap farce *Hotel Paradiso*.

Although these films were reasonably successful, she was being offered fewer and fewer high-quality American movies. Lollobrigida was the female lead in the limp 1968 Bob Hope comedy *The Private Navy of Sgt. O'Farrell* and had what was arguably her last impressive Hollywood role in *Buona Sera, Mrs. Campbell* (1969), a very funny sex-themed comedy that boasted a cast of Telly Savalas, Phil Silvers, Shelley Winters and Peter Lawford.

Above right: Gina's natural beauty helped launch her career at an early age.
Left: This Mexican lobby card for *Fanfan la Tulipe* (1952) appears to put the emphasis on La Lollo's bust over and above the film's other merits.
Opposite: Gina Lollobrigida's first American-produced film was *Trapeze*. Her role as Lola, a high-wire artist, gave ample opportunity for the producers to display her physical assets.

By the mid-Seventies, the plum roles had evaporated and so did Lollobrigida's commitment to acting. She had long had a private passion for sculpting and photography and devoted more time to these endeavours. Her work as a photographer won international acclaim and as a result she gained access to world leaders and celebrities. Their portraits formed the centre of exhibitions and books that documented her photographic skills.

Lollobrigida has only married once, to a Slovenian doctor, Mirko Skofic, who later became her manager and was executive producer on his wife's 1958 film, *Fast and Sexy*. They were married in 1949 and divorced in 1971. The couple had one child, a son. Lollobrigida's romances since then have been the stuff of gossip page fodder. She had affairs with numerous men, but has never remarried. In 2006, she announced her engagement to Javier Rigau y Rafols, a Spaniard who was 34 years younger than her. However, the Italian press made such a scandal of the issue that the couple never went through with the wedding.

Lollobrigida continued to act occasionally into the late 1990s, but the projects were all unmemorable. However, she did also dedicate herself to working for Italian-American causes and in 2008 was given the Lifetime Achievement Award from the National Italian American Foundation. Lollobrigida has also been awarded the Légion d'Honneur by France. In 1999, she ran unsuccessfully for a seat in the European parliament and in 2003 had a book published depicting her finest sculptures.

Lollobrigida has a reputation for being the ultimate diva and represents an era of glamour that is long gone from the film industry. She candidly assessed her own life: "I studied painting and sculpting at school and became an actress by mistake.... I've had many lovers and still have romances. I am very spoiled. All my life, I've had too many admirers."

Above: Frank Sinatra may have received top billing, but Gina stole the show in the war-time drama *Never So Few*.

Far left: *Hotel Paradiso*.

Left: Now in her early forties, Gina Lollobrigida was still as sexy as ever when she appeared in *Death Laid an Egg* (1968).

SOPHIA LOREN

Sophia Loren was born Sofia Villani Scicolone in Rome in 1934. From her humble beginnings, few could have guessed that one day she would become both an icon of international cinema and an Oscar winner, as well as one of cinema's most enduring beauties.

Loren was the child of an unmarried mother, who her father refused to marry. In desperate and impoverished circumstances, she and her younger sister, Maria, were taken by their mother to Pozzuoli, Italy, where her grandmother allowed them all to live with her. However, the Second World War wreaked havoc on the family. The town was bombed numerous times because of an ammunition factory nearby. For a while, the family relocated again to nearby Naples, only to return to Pozzuoli after the war, where the women set up an ad-hoc pub in their apartment to make ends meet.

In her autobiography, the actress wrote: "At fourteen my body miraculously came to life, virtually overnight, and by fourteen-and-a-half the ugly duckling had bloomed into a long-legged, full-breasted swan. It was as if I had burst from an egg and was born. For the first time in my life, when I walked down the street, I heard the mellifluous sound of male whistles." After moving back to Rome with her mother, Loren paid her way by posing for Fumetti photographs that appeared in Italian newspapers. (Fumetti are comic strips using photos rather than drawings.) During this time the young Loren captured the eye of future film producer Carlo Ponti (who was 37 at the time) when she became a finalist in a local beauty contest aged just 15.

The May/December romance was not a fleeting one and they would marry in 1957. However, Ponti had married previously and the Italian government did not recognise divorce, so the couple were technically living in sin. To avert a scandal and arrest on a bigamy charge, Loren and Ponti annulled their marriage in 1962, only to remarry three years later when divorce was decreed as a right under Italian law. In an industry in which marriages rarely last, Loren and Ponti were the exception. They had two sons and remained together until Ponti's death in 2007, since when Loren has kept to her vow that she could never love another man enough to marry him.

Loren's early career saw her make a meteoric rise. Following her work posing for both Fumetti and cheesecake photographs, she drew the attention of local casting agents, and in 1951 won – along with her mother – a bit part in MGM's epic *Quo Vadis*. She eventually gained name recognition through Italian films such as *It's Him!... Yes! Yes!* (1951), in which she was billed as Sofia Lazzaro, and went on to make *Two Nights With Cleopatra* (1953), by which time she had adopted the stage name of Sophia Loren. These two films would be the only time

the actress accepted roles where she was required to appear topless. Again, in her biography, she wrote: "In those days scenes were often shot specifically for the French version of a picture being made.

Censorship was far less restrictive in France, so the scenes could be more revealing. During the shooting of the scene in which I appeared in *It's Him!... Yes! Yes!* (1951), which involved several girls like myself in harem costume, the director asked that we do one take topless for the French version. The other girls obliged him and, after a moment's hesitation, I did too. It

was a quick take, and that was that, but I learned something about myself from that incident. I don't feel seductive or sexy when I expose myself to the camera. I feel awkward and childish. I think exposure is a debasement of the acting process because it removes the element of mystery."

Opposite: Loren's presence in *Boy on a Dolphin* is the primary reason the film is remembered at all today.
Top: *The Pride and the Passion.*
Below: Publicity still from *It's Him, Yes! Yes!* Nude scenes were filmed for the French version.

She earned critical acclaim that same year in a prestigious film production of *Aida*, in which she played the title role. Soon she was working with some of Italy's most respected directors, such as Vittorio De Sica. In 1954, she co-starred with Marcello Mastroianni for the first time in *Too Bad She's Bad*. The pair would become close personal friends and co-star numerous times over the years.

Hollywood began to take notice of the Italian beauty and Loren was lured to America by a lucrative multi-picture contract from Paramount Pictures. She made her American film début opposite Alan Ladd in *Boy on a Dolphin* (1957). The film was unremarkable in most respects, but publicity stills of Loren posing dripping wet in tight clothing took the world by storm and cemented her status as a leading sex symbol. That same year, Loren was the female lead in what should have been a blockbuster production: Stanley Kramer's *The Pride and the Passion*. Although she co-starred with Cary Grant and Frank Sinatra in this historical epic, both male leads were badly miscast and the film was a major failure. Loren, however, emerged unscathed, as she would again later that year when she co-starred in a rare John Wayne flop, *Legend of the Lost*. She also co-starred with Grant again in the comedy *Houseboat* (1958) and later confessed that the couple had a torrid affair, but ultimately she returned to Carlo Ponti.

In 1961, Loren's status in world cinema was raised even higher when she won the Academy Award for Best Actress in Vittorio De Sica's *Two Women* (1960), a sobering drama about the trials of a young mother and her daughter trying to survive as refugees in war-torn Italy. Loren was originally cast as the daughter, but lobbied the producers so extensively that they finally allowed her to play the mother.

Displaying an emotional range few thought was within her capabilities, Loren won numerous international awards and became the first person to win the Best Actress Oscar for a performance in a foreign language film. This was followed by a co-starring role alongside Charlton Heston in producer Samuel Bronston's epic blockbuster *El Cid*, also released in 1961. The film was an enormous critical and box-office success, but this time there were no romantic sparks between Loren and her leading man, as Heston accused her of indulging in diva-like behaviour and acting like a cold fish during their love scenes together.

Loren continued to switch between Italian films and Hollywood productions. She had major successes with *Boccaccio '70* (1962), *Yesterday, Today and Tomorrow* (1963) and *Marriage Italian Style* (1964) – the latter two with Mastroianni. Loren reunited with Samuel Bronston in 1964 for another epic, *The Fall of the Roman Empire*, but the film became a legendary disaster and virtually destroyed

Bronston's career. Loren at least had the solace of a million-dollar pay cheque.

Around this time, her box-office success in English-language films became quite chequered. Carlo Ponti cast her in what amounted to a cameo role (despite top billing) in the 1965 World War Two spy film *Operation Crossbow*, but the movie was a financial failure, notwithstanding a desperate attempt to reissue it under the awkward title *The Great Spy Mission*. Loren was also the female lead in the star-packed 1965 comedy *Lady L*, but even with a cast that included Paul Newman and David Niven the movie under-performed.

Another of her 'can't miss' films did just that when she starred alongside Marlon Brando in *A Countess From Hong Kong* (1967). Hyped as Charles Chaplin's return to the director's chair after a decade-long absence, critics attacked the film for being hopelessly dated – and, even worse, unfunny. Chaplin and Brando took most of the scorn and Loren once again emerged with her reputation intact. She exerted some box-office pull with the 1966 spy adventure *Arabesque* opposite Gregory Peck, but her most acclaimed work continued to be in Italian cinema. However, the mixed response to her films did not prevent her from receiving the Golden Globe Award as the world's most popular actress an astonishing four times during the 1960s.

Opposite: Few women can look this good in stockings and suspenders: *Lucky to Be a Woman* (1955).
Above left: Unusual press still from *Heller in Pink Tights* (1960).
Left and above right: On the set of *Legend of the Lost*.

Above: An on-set candid taken during the filming of
A Countess From Hong Kong.
Right: Surely the epitome of every man's dream…
The Millionairess (1960).
Far right: Only Loren could have made a scullery maid
and prostitute look so alluring. As Aldonza in *Man of
La Mancha*.
Opposite: Wearing a harem costume in the brothel
sequence from *Marriage Italian Style*.

In 1972, Loren was cast as Dulcinea in the big-budget musical version of *Man of La Mancha*, but the movie was a critical and box-office disaster. She also appeared in several other star-packed films that never lived up to their potential, including *The Cassandra Crossing* (1977), *Brass Target* (1978) and *Firepower* (1979). If Loren was losing her popularity with movie audiences, she was still a queen when it came to star power and the gossip magazines. In the Eighties and Nineties, Loren worked much more selectively, although she did appear in a 1980 TV dramatisation of her own life. She also suffered a personal scandal when she was convicted of tax evasion in Italy and served a brief jail sentence. The incident had no impact on her popularity and may have even enhanced it.

Loren also launched her own line of cosmetics, which proved highly successful. In the cinema, she had a late career hit with Jack Lemmon and Walter Matthau in *Grumpier Old Men* (1995). In the Nineties, Loren was accorded many honours, including a special Academy Award and Cecil B. DeMille Golden Globe Award in recognition of her extraordinary career. Today, she acts only sporadically, but did take a high-profile role in the 2009 screen adaptation of the play *Nine*. Loren was not out of place in the musical, as she has recorded a number of successful albums during her career. Still stunningly beautiful, as she proved in 2006 by becoming the oldest women to have posed for the famous Pirelli calendar, Sophia Loren remains the personification of the modern, liberated woman.

LUCiANA PALUZZi

If it had not been for a quirk of fate, one of Italy's most impressive sex symbols may have become a naval engineer. Instead, she pursued a career that saw her sharing the screen with both James Bond and The Men From U.N.C.L.E.

Her father was opposed to any suggestion that his beautiful daughter might pursue a career in the arts. However, during a dinner conversation with a friend, who was a production manager on the 1954 film *Three Coins in the Fountain*, it was explained that director Jean Negulesco was having a very difficult time casting the role of star Rossano Brazzi's younger sister. The man's eyes fell on gorgeous Luciana and he made the off-hand suggestion that she test for the part. Because her father trusted his friend's instincts, he gave his permission. Negulesco was suitably impressed and the young woman found herself, accompanied by her mother, shooting sequences in the Alps. Paluzzi decided there and then that the glamour of show business was irresistible. The Italian navy may have lost an engineer, but the film industry gained a new talent.

Paluzzi found herself in demand almost immediately. She deftly avoided the casting couch and proved she had the stamina and self-reliance to survive in an industry where young actresses often found that their careers were reliant upon how 'co-operative' they were with predatory producers. In 1956, she had a small role with Brigitte Bardot in the film *Mademoiselle Striptease*, and Paluzzi later recalled that Bardot had "a heart of gold". She made several films in Italy before emmigrating to England, where she won some prominent roles, even if the pictures themselves might have been forgettable. In the 1958 British-based Second World War yarn *Tank Force* (aka *No Time to Die*), she worked with producer Albert R. Broccoli and director Terence Young. The movie was nondescript, but the relationships with Broccoli and Young would pay major dividends a few years later.

Paluzzi also starred in *Sea Fury* (1958), another British adventure flick with up-and-coming stars Stanley Baker and Robert Shaw, and then alternated between Italian and British films. She signed a seven year contract with Rank, but accepted an offer to star in the 1960 American TV series *Five Fingers*, for which the producers bought out her contract. Despite the espionage-themed show only lasting seven episodes, Hollywood came calling again the following year. Paluzzi was now under contract to Fox and she landed a supporting role in the star-studded melodrama *Return to Peyton Place*, directed by actor José Ferrer.

Although Paluzzi was determined to make her mark as a serious dramatic actress, one of her most popular roles during this period was in the 1964 comedy *Muscle Beach Party* alongside Annette Funicello and Frankie Avalon. The film

was a box-office hit, though Paluzzi realised there was little need to clear mantle space for an Oscar.

In the early-to-mid-Sixties, Paluzzi made guest appearances on a number of popular

American television shows. She had a small but memorable role in the 1964 pilot episode of *The Man From U.N.C.L.E.*, playing a double-dealing secret agent who tries to use her seduction skills to assassinate Robert Vaughn's Napoleon Solo. The two-part episode was

released theatrically in 1966 as *To Trap a Spy*. In 1965, Paluzzi auditioned for the role of Domino, the female lead in the James Bond film *Thunderball*. The director, Terence Young, had invited her to try out for the part. Despite his influence (and the fact that another old friend, Albert R. Broccoli, was producing), Paluzzi was told she hadn't got the role. Her disappointment was short-lived, however, when Young informed her that she'd won the part of the 'bad girl', Fiona Volpe. Paluzz's bedtime antics with Sean Connery's James Bond remain among the series' most memorable scenes.

The Bond publicity bandwagon thrust Paluzzi and her fellow female co-stars Claudine Auger and Martine Beswick into the international spotlight, with their faces gracing magazine covers worldwide. However, some major Italian directors she had hoped to work with felt that her 'Bond Girl' image meant audiences wouldn't accept her in more challenging roles. Nevertheless, she remained in-demand, and co-starred in films like *The Venetian Affair* (1967), which reunited her with Robert Vaughn, and the 1967 Western *Chuka*, in which she appeared with Rod Taylor and Ernest Borgnine.

Paluzzi had divorced her husband, actor Brett Halsey, in 1962 and throughout the sixties needed money to raise their son, resulting in her accepting lesser movies like the 1968 science fiction film *The Green Slime*. Although she continued to find work, the quality of both the films and roles began to diminish, as evidenced by *99 Women* (1969) and *The Sensuous Nurse* (1975), to name but two. In 1979 she met Michael Solomon, a former United Artists executive who, upon seeing Paluzzi in *Thunderball* had made a vow to marry her. Introduced at a party, he made good on the promise and the couple were married in 1979. (Terence Young, who became a devoted friend, gave her away at their wedding.)

Solomon became a major innovator in the development of TV syndication and the couple led a jet-set lifestyle. Paluzzi therefore felt she could not adequately concentrate on her acting career and went into self-imposed retirement. Today, she and Solomon live the high life in a beautiful home in the Hollywood hills. However, she confesses to occasionally missing her career as an actress and periodically attends autograph fairs to meet her enduring legion of fans.

Opposite: Angela, Napoleon Solo's nemesis, in the first *Man From U.N.C.L.E.* movie *To Trap a Spy*.
Top: *Sea Fury*.

ELKE SOMMER

Stunningly beautiful Elke Sommer was born during the turbulent years of the Second World War. Embarking on a modeling career as a teenager, she would work with celebrated director Vittoria De Sica, star in an Inspector Clouseau film and grace the pages of *Playboy*.

Elke Sommer was born Elke Schletz in Berlin, Germany in 1940. After much of the city was reduced to rubble, they resettled in Erlangen, a small town in picturesque southern Germany. Sommer's father, a Lutheran minister, died when she was only 14 years old, at which point the attractive young girl found herself having to make adult decisions about her future. She emigrated to England, where she worked for a time as an au pair girl, before returning to Germany to continue her education. At this point she entered modeling, becoming a popular pin-up girl thanks in no small part to her willingness to pose semi-naked. Sommer's stunning beauty inevitably led to film work, though originally only in small roles. She won a beauty contest in Italy and caught the eye of Vittoria De Sica, who cast her in the 1960 movie *Men and Noblemen*. The following year, she had great success playing the starring role in the erotic thriller *Daniella by Night*, as well as taking a leading part in the British comedy *Don't Bother to Knock?* opposite Richard Todd.

For the next few years, Sommer was a rising star in European movies. In 1963 she was prominently cast in Carl Foreman's controversial Second World War film *The Victors*. Suddenly, Hollywood came beckoning and she starred with Paul Newman and Edward G. Robinson in the hit Hitchcockian thriller *The Prize* (1963). For her performance, she was given the Golden Globe Award for Most Promising Female Newcomer. The following year she won her most important role to date, appearing as the female lead in *The Pink Panther* sequel *A Shot in the Dark* opposite Peter Sellers. The film was an enormous success with both the critics and the public, and Sommer had proven she was as adept at light comedy as she was at drama.

In 1964, Sommer became romantically involved with famed Hollywood entertainment writer Joe Hyams and they married that year. They remained together until their divorce in 1981. Sommer's new-found fame didn't preclude her from posing for *Playboy* and she was featured in pictorials in 1964 and 1967. She also developed a passion for painting and, in between films, devoted much of her time to exploring her talent. Sommer continued to appear in major studio productions of varying quality throughout the 1960s. *The Oscar* (1966) has gathered a cult following in the same vein as *Valley of the Dolls* as one of those Hollywood star-packed misfires that is so bad it's good. Similarly, the Bob Hope farce *Boy, Did I Get a Wrong Number!* (1966) was an undistinguished vehicle for her talents.

Like most actresses during the Sixties, Sommer benefited from the spy movie craze, co-starring with Robert Vaughn in the 1967 espionage thriller *The Venetian Affair* and appearing opposite Robert Stack in *The Corrupt Ones* (1967, aka *The Peking Medallion*). Perhaps her most memorable spy movie role was with Sylva Koscina as a deadly duo of femme fatales in the Bulldog Drummond adventure *Deadlier Than the Male* (1967). She also acted with Dean Martin in *The Wrecking Crew* (1969), the last entry in the Matt Helm series.

As the Sixties drew to a close, her film *The Wicked Dreams of Paula Schultz* (1968) was lambasted by critics as a vulgar sex comedy hiding behind the trappings of a family film, not least because the male leads, Bob Crane, Werner Klemperer and John Banner, were the stars of the popular TV series *Hogan's Heroes*. That same year, Sommer starred with Gary Lockwood in the caper movie *They Came to Rob Las Vegas*, a European film that received a major release in America and won respectable notices. However, Sommer's days making major Hollywood productions were over and

henceforth she would work almost entirely in European-based films. These included the First World War movie *Zeppelin* (1971), the cult British sex comedy *Percy* (1971), and director Mario Bava's horror films *Baron Blood* (1972) and *Lisa and the Devil* (1972), the latter co-starring Telly Savalas and Sylva Koscina. Sommer also appeared in the star-studded 1974 remake of Agatha Christie's *Ten Little Indians* (also known as *And Then There Were None*). In 1975, she featured in Peter Rogers' British farce *Carry on Behind*, earning the highest sum paid to an actress in the long-running series.

In the ensuing years, Sommer has worked periodically in films and on television. When interviewed in 2007 about her typecasting as a sex siren during this era, she replied: "It did make it more difficult later on to be taken seriously as a dramatic actress. At the time, however, I didn't think about it that much or take it into consideration. It was the same fate that affected Brigitte Bardot, who I admired tremendously. She was always cast as the French 'sex kitten'. Look at Marilyn Monroe. She was so talented but all everyone saw was mouth, lashes, tits and ass. Yet, she had something quite extraordinary. I would like to have met her."

She made the news in 1993 when she won a libel suit against Zsa Zsa Gabor, which resulted in her being paid over $1 million in damages. The bizarre dispute occurred when Sommer suggested that Ms Gabor had such a plump bottom she would need assistance getting on a horse. Gabor responded by telling the press that Sommer was going bald and was so destitute that she had to earn money by knitting sweaters. The jury agreed Sommer had been defamed and she collected a sizeable cheque for damages.

Since 1993, Sommer has been married to successful hotelier Wolf Walther. The couple live in California, where Sommer spends much of her time painting. In recent years she has also travelled with a one-woman stage show and occasionally can be persuaded to sing in public. Sommer, who speaks several different languages fluently, has had a number of successful albums released in Europe. One of the more unusual aspects of her legacy is that she continues to insist that the Hollywood home she shared with Joe Hyams was haunted.

Top: *Deadlier Than the Male.*
Opposite: Stunning on-location portrait from *The Wrecking Crew.*

BARBARA STEELE

Born in England in 1938, Barbara Steele has an enduring following largely due to her appearances in cult horror films. In particular, her role in Mario Bava's *Black Sunday* showcased her mysterious persona and exotic physical appearance, in the process making her an international celebrity.

Steele was originally placed under contract to Rank, but appeared only in small, largely forgotten British films. She was next under contract to Fox, but her introduction to Hollywood filmmaking suffered a severe setback when she argued with director Don Siegel on the set of the Elvis Presley Western *Flaming Star* (1960). Most aspiring actresses would have been thrilled to be hired as the love interest in a Presley film, but the fiercely independent Steele walked off the set. Her role was assumed by Barbara Eden. Having sabotaged her own career with the major studios, Steele willingly took the lead in Italian director Mario Bava's 1960 horror film *Black Sunday* and the course of her career was irrevocably changed.

However, the success of *Black Sunday* was a double-edged sword, as Steele found little enthusiasm among producers for casting her in non-horror properties. Instead, she became synonymous with the genre. In 1961 she scored another success as the scheming wife of Vincent Price in producer Roger Corman's film adaptation of Edgar Allan Poe's *The Pit and the Pendulum*. The movie's success simply cemented her typecasting, as did the following year's hit *The Horrible Dr. Hichcock*.

She was also cast in a supporting role in Fellini's 1963 masterpiece *8½*, but parts in mainstream films did not come. A string of Italian horror films followed and Steele found herself working for many of the leading cult directors: Riccardo Freda on *The Ghost* (1963), Antonio Margheriti on both *Castle of Blood* (1964) and *The Long Hair of Death* (1964), and Michael Reeves in *The She-Beast* (1966). A rare change of pace was provided by a young German filmmaker, Volker Schlöndorff, who cast her in *The Young Torless* (1966).

Her husband, screenwriter James Poe (to whom she was married between 1969 and 1978), specifically wrote a breakthrough role for her in the acclaimed 1969 film *They Shoot Horses, Don't They?* However, she suffered disappointment when director Sydney Pollack opted for a bigger box-office name and cast Susannah York in the part. In 1974, Steele made a memorable impression as a wheelchair-bound warden in the 'women-in-prison' exploitation film *Caged Heat,* an early effort by director Jonathan Demme, and in David Cronenberg's *Shivers*.

At the same time, Steele kept striving for work in non-exploitation films. She landed roles in more serious movies like *I Never Promised You a Rose Garden* (1977) and Louis Malle's *Pretty Baby* (1978), but the parts did not provide any showcase moments. In 1978, Steele found more success in the genre she had come to resent, playing a key role in director Joe Dante's hit horror satire *Piranha*. She also scored with the 1979 horror film *Silent Scream.*

Perhaps improbably, Steele expanded her career to a major role behind the cameras, co-producing the highly acclaimed Emmy award-winning 1983 mini-series *The Winds of War* in conjunction with legendary producer Dan Curtis. She reunited with Curtis to produce the equally epic 1988 sequel *War and Remembrance.* In 1991, she had a one-season run on the popular TV soap opera *Dark Shadows*, a remake of the well-remembered Dan Curtis TV series and which inevitably had a horror story premise. Today, Steele seems to have reached a level of comfort with her fame and enduring popularity that stem from the horror genre. She acts in and produces the occasional project, but vows that her goal is to "never climb out of another fucking coffin again!"

Top: *Black Sunday.*
Left: *The Maniacs* (1964) was a humorous look at Italian society from future horror director Lucio Fulci, with Steele at the height of her vampy deliciousness.
Opposite: Bewitching in Roger Corman's *The Pit and the Pendulum.*

THE CONTINENTALS ROUND-UP

There are a great many other 'Continental ladies' who demand our attention, including Swedish-born actress Essy Persson, Italian stars Laura Antonelli and Stefania Sandrelli, Bond girl Claudine Auger, *Black Emmanuelle*'s Laura Gemser, the Israeli-born Daliah Lavi and Jane Birkin, who although born in England forged her acting career in France.

Although Essy Persson starred in many sexually charged films, her career highlight was undoubtedly *Therese and Isabelle*, the respected 1968 film directed by Radley Metzger which explored two young girls' foray into lesbianism. However, she is probably better known for the 1965 drama *I, a Woman*, playing Viv, a young girl who is as sexually adventurous as any man she encounters in her life. It was one of the first sexually themed films from Sweden to gain a wide release in America, and a surprise box-office hit. Persson's only 'internationally-made' picture was the Vincent Price horror flick, *Cry of the Banshee* (1970). Her last-known role came

in a 1983 Swedish TV series called *Profitorerna*.

Italian actress Laura Antonelli first appeared in Italian advertisements for Coca Cola before entering show business in 1965, an early film role finding her in the Vincent Price secret agent comedy spoof *Dr. Goldfoot and the Girl Bombs* (1966). Another interesting early picture is Massimo Dallamano's *Venus in Furs* (1969), which was also titled *Devil in the Flesh*. Antonelli appeared in the Hollywood Western *A Man Called Sledge* in 1970, but her career continued mainly in Italian-made productions, especially sex farces. Her breakthrough role was as the housekeeper Angela in *Malicious* (1973), which

featured many on-screen sexual barriers being broken, including one scene where Angela rapes the teenage son of the man she is about to marry.

Antonelli was later cast in Visconti's final film, *The Innocent* (1976), and continued to act until 1991, when she was convicted of cocaine possession after police raided her home. Sentenced to house arrest, the actress never stopped professing her innocence. After a series of appeals that extended a full decade, the court overturned the conviction. The experience seemed to diminish Antonelli's desire for the spotlight. She now lives in quiet retirement, but remains one of the era's more notable screen sex kittens.

Opposite top: Claudine Auger in *That Man George!* (1966).
Opposite below: A tender moment between Therese (Essy Persson) and Isabelle (Anna Gaël) in the schoolgirl lesbian love story *Therese and Isabelle*.
Left and top left: The allure of a more mature woman. The stunning Laura Antonelli in *Malicious*.
Top right: A German lobby card for *Mission Stardust* (1967).

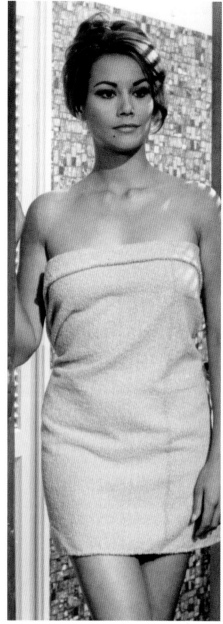

Above: The sex comedy *Anyone Can Play* teamed Auger with fellow ex-Bond girl Ursula Andress.
Right: Claudine Auger.
Above right and opposite: Following her role in *Thunderball*, Claudine Auger starred in another spy thriller, this time *That Man George!*

Claudine Auger has strong James Bond roots, having played the female lead Domino in *Thunderball* (1965). However, that remained her main claim to international fame, as the majority of her career was spent working in European cinema. Born Claudine Oger in 1941, she won the title of Miss France Monde and, at the age of just 17, was the first runner-up in the 1958 Miss World contest. Auger studied acting at the Paris Drama Conservatory and made her big screen début in an uncredited blink-and-you'll-miss-her part in the 1959 Romy Schneider/Alain Delon romance *Christine*. Although still uncredited, she had a more prominent part in Cocteau's *The Testament of Orpheus* (1959).

At age 18 Auger married film director Pierre Gaspard-Huit, who was 24 years her senior, and starred in two of his films: *The Iron Mask* (1962) and *The Vengeance of Kali* (1963). James Bond director Terence Young suggested she test for the part of Domino after spotting her while on holiday in Nassau, and she worked for him again in the World War Two spy thriller *Triple Cross* in 1966. In 1967, *Anyone Can Play* saw Auger teamed with Ursula Andress, Marisa Mell and Virna Lisa in a sex comedy, and she also had the female lead in Alain Jessau's *Jeu de Massacre* (1967).

From this point on she predominantly worked in French and Italian cinema. She was seen in the all-star giallo *The Black Belly of the Tarantula* alongside Barbara Bouchet, Stefania Sandrelli and future Bond girl Barbara Bach, plus she starred in Mario Bava's slasher template *Bay of Blood* (1970). Auger married again, this time to businessman Peter Brent, who passed away in 2008.

In 1997, Claudine Auger decided to retire from the screen. Unlike many of her peers, she has remained out of the public eye and never attends 007 premieres or related events. Brent once told the authors that Auger had no interest in discussing her past and generally refused to do interviews, thus heightening her air of mystery.

Although Sylvia Kristel is world-famous for her portrayal of *Emmanuelle*, it is Laura Gemser who must be crowned 'Queen of the Sequels'. Born in Indonesia, Gemser was brought up in the Netherlands from the age of four. After studying art at school, she first gained attention working as a nude model in men's magazines. Following a move to Italy in the Seventies, Gemser secured a small part in *Emmanuelle II* (1975), before really launching her softcore exploitation career playing the title role in *Black Emanuelle* the same year.

Although she made other films, Gemser appeared in nine sequels (two without the name Emanuelle in the title), one of the more infamous being *Emanuelle and the Last Cannibals* (1977), directed by Joe D'Amato and featuring excessive scenes of cannibal violence. She had the female lead in Michael Landon's 1983 TV movie *Love is Forever* (directed by Hall Bartlett), but was credited as Moira Chen, a name she has used occasionally throughout her career. In less than 20 years Gemser appeared in 57 films and occasionally worked behind the scenes as a costume designer. She retired in the early Nineties and still lives in Italy.

With her pouty good looks, Stefania Sandrelli has developed a devoted following among

Emanuelle Nera

愛のエマニエル

international movie-lovers. Born in 1946 in Viareggio, Italy, Sandrelli – like many of her peers – came to the attention of the film industry after she won a beauty contest at age 15. In 1961, she had an early role with legendary actor Ugo Tognazzi in *The Fascist* and the same year won a more prominent part as a teenage vixen opposite the great Marcello Mastroianni in the hit film *Divorce – Italian Style*. Sandrelli has been a popular presence in Italian cinema ever since.

Her other major movies include Pietro Germi's *Seduced and Abandoned* (1964), two classics for director Bernardo Bertolucci in *The Conformist* (1970) and *1900* (1976), the cult giallo *The Black Belly of the Tarantula* (1971, co-starring with Claudine Auger, Barbara Bouchet and Barbara Bach), *Alfredo, Alfredo* (1972, with Dustin Hoffman), and, in her most famous role, director Tinto Brass's titillating *The Key* (1983). Her performance in the latter, which required her to appear in explicit sex scenes totally naked aged 37, ensured her iconic status in Italian cinema. Sandrelli has since worked non-stop both in feature films and on television, gaining a new generation of fans through her remarkable legacy in movies like Bigas Luna's *Jamon Jamon* (1992) and Bernardo Bertolucci's *Stealing Beauty* (1996).

LAURA GEMSER
Emmanuelle
EVA NEGRA
JACK PALANCE

Opposite above: Although far removed from the original, *Black Emanuelle* introduced the beautiful Laura Gemser to the world. Most territories would have avoided the nudity seen in the Japanese poster.
Opposite below: The use of the wicker furniture and style of the lettering might imply it's an *Emmanuelle* film, but *Eva Negra* was the Argentinian title for *Black Cobra Woman* (1976). However, there was certainly no shortage of female nudity.
Above and left: Tinto Brass's *The Key* was one of the most explicit films actress Stefania Sandrelli appeared in. The highly erotic story of a husband and wife's sexual encounters required full frontal nudity.

Although strongly associated with French pop culture and cinema, Jane Birkin is actually a native of Britain, having been born in London in 1946. Birkin's doe-eyed innocent look, combined with an air of smouldering sexuality, meant she became a prominent part of the London scene in the mid-Sixties. She appeared in two popular counter-culture films, Richard Lester's *The Knack… and How to Get It* (1965) and more prominently in Michelangelo Antonioni's controversial classic *Blowup* (1966).

In London, Birkin was romanced by film composer John Barry and the couple wed in 1965, a union that lasted for three years. She never had a 'breakthrough' role but built a strong following for her music, particularly her frequent collaborations with Serge Gainsbourg, whom she married in 1969. Their steamy recording of 'Je T'Aime… Moi Non Plus' that same year set off a firestorm of controversy due to its sexual content, which included Birkin feigning an orgasm. The song was banned on many British and European radio stations, even as it climbed the charts.

Birkin had a memorable role as Brigitte Bardot's lesbian lover in the provocative 1973 film *Don Juan (Or If Don Juan Were a Woman)*. She also made rare appearances in two major Hollywood productions based on Agatha Christie thrillers, *Death on the Nile* (1978) and *Evil Under the Sun* (1982). In recent years, Birkin has worked steadily in film, TV and on stage.

The Israeli-born beauty Daliah Lavi entered the world in 1942. A chance encounter with Kirk Douglas, who was making a film in Israel, led to his taking the ten-year old Lavi under his wing and arranging a scholarship so she could study ballet in Sweden. With her dark, striking good looks, Lavi ultimately decided to become an actress. She appeared in a number of non-English language films before Douglas rescued her again by casting Lavi in a prominent role in his 1962 film *Two Weeks in Another Town*. Lavi continued acting in European films and proved a striking presence in Mario Bava's cult horror film *The Whip and the Body* (1963). She had another high-profile English-language role in the 1965 production of *Lord Jim* (which landed her the cover of the prestigious *Saturday Evening Post* in America), which Lavi followed with the enjoyable Agatha Christie adaptation *Ten Little Indians* (1965).

During this period she became synonymous with the spy movie craze, making two memorable appearances in 1966. Firstly, in stockings and suspenders in *The Spy With a Cold Nose* (1966), and then opposite Dean Martin in the first Matt Helm film, *The Silencers*. The following year, Lavi gained even greater fame in the mega-budget, all-star fiasco *Casino Royale*. Curiously, although she is billed in the credits as 'The Detainer', Lavi's character's name is never mentioned throughout the entire film. Her most memorable scene sees her tied naked to an operating table by bumbling would-be megalomaniac Jimmy Bond (Woody Allen).

Lavi next appeared in the Harry Alan Towers comedy *Rocket to the Moon* (1967) and capped off the Sixties with two more spy movies, *Nobody Runs Forever* (1968, aka *The High Commissioner*) and *Some Girls Do* (1969). Her last big screen appearance was in the 1971 Yul Brynner Western *Catlow*. Unbeknownst to many movie fans, she emerged as one of Germany's most popular singers in the Seventies. Lavi still records today, although she prefers to stay out of the spotlight and live a quiet life with her husband in America.

Opposite above: Two icons of French cinema, Jane Birkin and Brigitte Bardot, in *Don Juan (Or If Don Juan Were a Woman)*. However, few people at the time realised Birkin was, in fact, British.
Opposite below: Simply credited as 'The Blonde' in *Blowup*, Michelangelo's examination of the London fashion scene, Jane Birkin was soon much in demand by producers looking for a fresh new face.
Above left: The gorgeous Daliah Lavi.
Above right: Already a star in Europe by the time she made *The Spy with a Cold Nose*, Daliah Lavi appeared in six major spy themed films between 1966 and 1969.

MADE iN ENGLAND: BRiT GLAMOUR

The Sixties and Seventies was a rapidly changing period for the depiction of sex on film. By the Seventies, cinemas were awash with films exploitating the female form, from horror films, such as those made by Hammer and their competitors, to comedies, particularly the hugely successful *Carry On*, *Confessions* and *Adventures of...* series.

Audiences were offered an abundance of titillation and double entendres. Actresses who were prepared to display their assets were almost guaranteed full-time employment in an industry that was constantly on the verge of crisis and anxiously looking over its shoulder at the perceived threat of television. Both established actresses and models from the glamour industry were popping up (or more accurately out!) in such films on a regular basis.

Prior to this era, the 'sex sirens' of the British scene had been serious actresses who were as glamorous as they were overtly sexual: stars such as Diana Dors, Joan Collins, Shirley Anne Field and Sylvia Syms. Diana Dors was perhaps

the most famous, being presented as Britain's answer to Marilyn Monroe. Born Diana Mary Fluck in 1931, Dors studied at the London Academy of Music and Dramatic Arts, and was under contract to the Rank Organisation by the time she was 16. It has been reported that she once said of her name change: "They asked me to change my surname. I suppose they were afraid that if my real name 'Fluck' was up in lights and one of the bulbs blew…" Often cast in roles where men took advantage of her, Dors' best part was also one of her least glamorous – that of a murderess in *Yield to the Night* (1956). Although she became famous for her dyed blonde hair and busty appearance, she was,

in fact, a very good actress and made over 60 films, both in England and America. Sadly, towards the end of her career Dors began appearing in softcore sex comedies and, like her American contemporaries Monroe and Mansfield, died at an early age, in her case 52.

Top: *The Long Haul (1957)*.
Below: *Blonde Sinner* was the American title for *Yield to the Night*. Hardly apparent from the poster, but this was a serious film loosely based on the life of Ruth Ellis, the last woman to be hung in Britain.
Opposite: Britain's answer to Jayne Mansfield and Marilyn Monroe, and looking every inch a sex goddess. Diana Dors in *I Married a Woman* (1958).

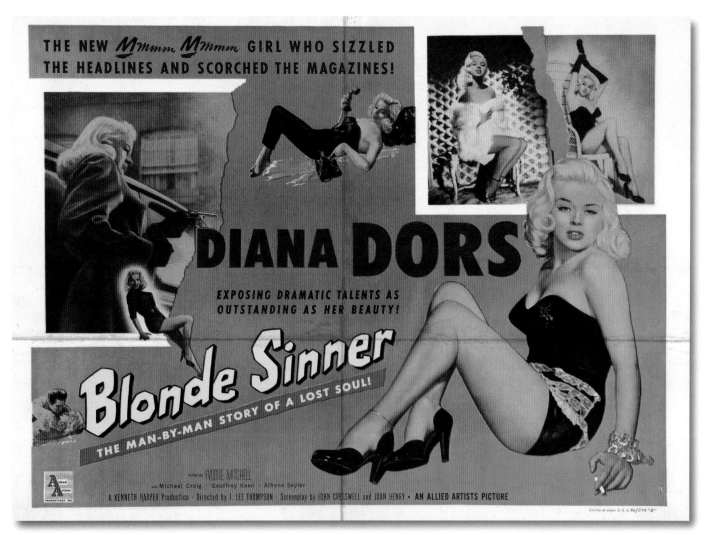

Top left: When it came to publicity, Joan Collins was the queen of exploitation, as seen here in *Rally 'Round the Flag Boys* (1958).
Above left: Joan Collins at 22 years of age and already starring in a major Hollywood film, as Princess Nellifer in *Land of the Pharaohs* (1955).
Right and opposite: Joan Collins' nude scenes caused a sensation at the box office in both *The Stud* and *The Bitch*.

Joan Collins, born in 1933, was the daughter of a successful show-business agent and led a fairly privileged life as a child, although she deplored her father's strict disciplinary measures. When only 17 years-old, Collins signed a contract with the J. Arthur Rank film company and was deemed 'the next big thing'. However, despite appearing in a number of popular films, she was primarily known as a pin-up girl, her face frequently gracing the covers of UK gossip magazines. Disgruntled with Rank's handling of her career, Collins signed with Fox and broadened her appeal outside of England. Though none of her films were particularly memorable, she worked consistently with some of the industry's biggest stars, such as Gregory Peck and Paul Newman, and guest starred on leading TV shows like *Batman*, *Star Trek*, *The Man from U.N.C.L.E.* and *The Persuaders*. In the late 1970s, Collins starred in film versions of her sister Jackie Collins' best-sellers (dubbed 'bonkbusters') *The Stud* (1978) and *The Bitch* (1979). Both were major box-office successes thanks to their blatant sexual content and advertising. Collins was a popular presence on major TV series as well, and in the Eighties landed the most prominent role of her career as 'bad girl' Alexis Colby in the TV series *Dynasty*. She also followed in her sister's footsteps and authored best-selling novels. Having been honoured with an OBE, Collins is now with her fifth husband and devotes considerable time to charitable works.

Above: Deemed too racy by the censors, Sylvia Syms'
cleavage, seen here in a posed publicity still, was
covered up in *Ice Cold in Alex*. John Mills doesn't
seem to mind…
Right: Laurence Harvey and the ravishing Sylvia Syms
on the backlot of Shepperton Studios during the
making of Val Guest's *Expresso Bongo*.
Far right: Looking seductive as Liz Ferrers, Sylvia Syms
provided the love interest in *Ferry to Hong Kong*.
Opposite left: Shirley Eaton.
Opposite right: Generally known for her 'girl-next-door'
roles before she made *Goldfinger*, Shirley Eaton was
the main female character in Mickey Spillane's *The
Girl Hunters* (1963) and featured prominently in the
film's ad campaign, as seen here on an American
poster.

Another recipient of the OBE is Sylvia Syms. Born in 1934, Syms attended RADA and made a splash of sorts playing a delinquent in the 1954 drama *My Teenage Daughter* (aka *Teenage Bad Girl*), which led to steady film work. In 1958, she co-starred with three male heavyweights – John Mills, Harry Andrews and Anthony Quayle – in the classic war movie *Ice Cold in Alex*. Soon, Syms was working with the likes of William Holden, Orson Welles, Dirk Bogarde and Patrick McGoohan in such quality films as *Ferry to Hong Kong* (1959), *Expresso Bongo* (1959), *The World of Suzie Wong* (1960), *Victim* (1961) and *The Quare Fellow* (1962).

She has been nominated for BAFTA awards three times, for *Woman in a Dressing Gown* (1957), *No Trees in the Street* (1958) and *The Tamarind Seed* (1974). Syms other major films include *Absolute Beginners* (1986), *Shirley*

Valentine (1989), *What a Girl Wants* (2003) and *The Queen* (2006), in which she played the Queen Mother. She has also portrayed Prime Minister Margaret Thatcher in acclaimed performances on TV and stage.

Shirley Eaton has the distinction of having created one of the most iconic images in motion picture history, when playing the ill-fated Jill Masterson, murdered and gilded with gold paint in the 1964 James Bond classic *Goldfinger*. Although she's only on-screen for a relatively short time, the role landed Eaton the cover of *Life* magazine and helped send the Bond film through the stratosphere.

A British native, Eaton was born in 1937. Her blonde hair combined with a fabulous figure resulted in a contract from Alexander Korda in the 1950s. Although trained in music and dance, Eaton had few opportunities to utilise these talents, as she was generally cast in

popular but lightweight ventures like *Doctor in the House* (1954), *Three Men in a Boat* (1956), *Doctor at Large* (1957), *What a Carve Up!* (1961) and several of the *Carry On* films. Following her international breakthrough with *Goldfinger*, Eaton appeared in *Rhino!* (1964), *Ten Little Indians* (1965), *Around the World Under the Sea* (1966) and *The Million Eyes of Su-Muru* (1967), amongst others.

Like many other actresses of the period, she then decided to quit her profession to concentrate on raising a family. (She was married to building contractor Colin Rowe from 1957 until his death in 1994.) Eaton remained in self-imposed retirement until the 1990s, when she became a popular fixture at autograph fairs in England. In 1999 she published her autobiography, *Golden Girl*, and still attends premieres of the latest 007 films.

Born in 1938, Shirley Anne Field was another popular British actress who came to prominence in the 1960s. She had been brought up in an orphanage when her mother had proved unable to care properly for Shirley and her brother, before becoming a successful glamour model. The film industry soon beckoned. Field appeared in a number of undistinguished films in the Fifties before being cast in supporting roles in *Horrors of the Black Museum* (1959), Michael Powell's controversial *Peeping Tom* (1960) and the rebel youth drama *Beat Girl* (1960).

Two further prominent parts followed when she appeared opposite Laurence Olivier in *The Entertainer* (1960) and then landed the female lead in director Tony Richardson's classic 'kitchen sink' drama *Saturday Night and Sunday Morning* (1960). Field was directed by Joseph Losey in the sci-fi classic *The Damned* (1961, aka *These Are the Damned*), provided the love interest for both Steve McQueen and Robert Wagner in *The War Lover* (1962) and starred with Yul Brynner in *Kings of the Sun* (1963). The comedy-drama *Alfie* (1966) starring Michael Caine afforded Field one of her final prominent roles of the decade.

She turned down repeated overtures from producer Albert R. Broccoli to be a 'Bond Girl'. Field almost dropped out of acting for over a decade, but among her more notable later films are *My Beautiful Laundrette* (1985) and *Hear My Song* (1991), in which she co-starred with old friend David McCallum. In 1991, she published her autobiography and today Field concentrates on her one-woman stage appearances in which she light-heartedly discusses her career.

Many actresses during the Sixties and Seventies became semi-famous for their figures, including busty ex-Harrison Marks glamour model Margaret Nolan. She was the *Goldfinger* poster campaign figurehead, as well as the model whose golden body appears in the famous opening credits. Nolan was also a regular in the *Carry On* films. Playing either a pub wench, farmer's daughter or servant girl, her role usually demanded she lose her clothes and display her more than ample cleavage on every occasion. Her bust became her trademark, though today she understandably prefers to be known as an 'actress' rather than for her chest measurements. Nolan has also gained a reputation as a talented painter.

The increasing popularity of British sexploitation comedy films brought to the screen the charms of Luan Peters, Imogen Hassell, Dana Gillespie and Kate O'Mara, to name but a few. Of course, none were really big star names. However, some, like Valerie Leon, Madeline Smith and Caroline Munro, carved an identifiable niche for themselves and developed loyal fan bases that still continue today.

Opposite: Shirley Anne Field.
Above: Her cups runneth over. Margaret Nolan delighting her male fans in *Carry On Girls* (1973).
Left: A small part for a big girl. Margaret Nolan played one of the voluptuous barmaids in the Michael Reeves horror classic *Witchfinder General* (1968, aka *The Conqueror Worm*).

SUSAN GEORGE

Born in England in 1950, Susan George began acting almost as soon as she could walk. Her gorgeous looks virtually guaranteed that she would fulfil her dream and become a professional actress. It would eventually lead to her career-defining role in Sam Peckinpah's *Straw Dogs*.

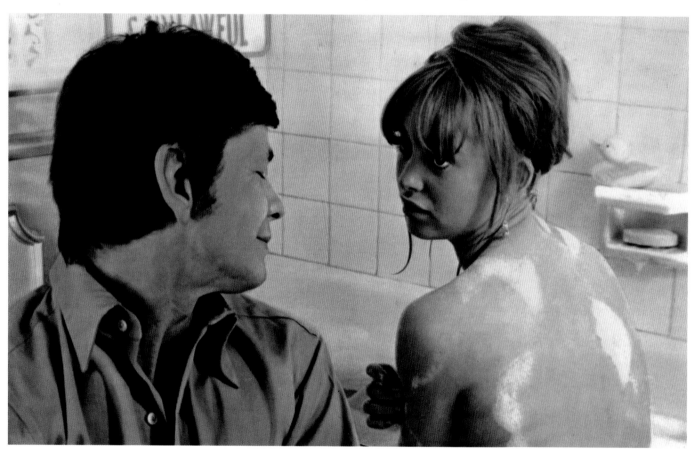

In the mid-Sixties, George had followed a familiar path, taking bit roles in largely undistinguished movies, although she did briefly appear in two notable 1967 movies: Ken Russell's Harry Palmer thriller *Billion Dollar Brain* and Michael Reeves' *The Sorcerers*. By the following year, she had been cast in the lead role in the cult comedy *All Neat in Black Stockings*, and followed this success with Peter Collinson's *Up the Junction* (1967). George was suddenly one of the 'it' girls, helped immeasurably by a plethora of publicity stills showing her clad in a trendy mini skirt. Over the next two years she co-starred with Christopher Jones in the Cold War adventure *The Looking Glass War* (1969), played a 16-year-old girl involved in a May/December romance with Charles Bronson in *Twinky* (1969, aka *Lola*) and appeared in John Hough's thriller *Eyewitness* (1970), also starring Mark Lester and Lionel Jeffries.

In 1971, George landed the most important role of her career, playing Dustin Hoffman's wife in director Sam Peckinpah's blood-and-guts suspense drama *Straw Dogs*. She and Hoffman starred as a couple trying to find happiness by relocating to what they believe is a quaint English village. Instead, they find their lives in danger from the menacing locals. A scene in which George's character is gang-raped was particularly controversial, largely because she appears to be a willing participant. Major stardom failed to materialise, however, although George worked steadily both in films and on TV, appearing in popular series like *The Persuaders!* with Roger Moore and Tony Curtis.

She re-teamed with director John Hough to star with Peter Fonda in the cult car chase film *Dirty Mary Crazy Larry* (1974). Clearly made for the drive-in movie circuit, the film was a big hit with its intended audience. The following year, George starred in the racially charged American Civil War drama *Mandingo*, which

although roundly panned by critics was a major success at the box office. Unfortunately, the quality of the roles declined as the Seventies wore on, as evidenced by *Out of Season* (1975), *A Small Town in Texas* (1976) and the Italian *Jaws* rip-off *Tintorera* (1977), all of which required nudity, something for which George was becoming well known.

George's romantic life often made the gossip columns, as she dated such diverse men as singer Andy Gibb and footballer George Best, as well as Prince Charles. In 1984 she married actor Simon MacCorkindale and they remained a devoted couple until his death in 2010. Susan George only acts sporadically today, preferring to spend much of her time breeding Arabian horses on the stud farm she owns in England.

Above: Susan George played a 16-year-old schoolgirl who marries a middle-aged writer of pornographic novels (Charles Bronson) in *Twinky*.

SUZY KENDALL

A popular leading lady when London was at the height of the 'mod' fashion in the Sixties, Suzy Kendall appeared in a wide variety of films. Born Frieda Harrison in 1944 in Belper, Derbyshire, the gorgeous Kendall specialised in playing innocent beauties often caught up in remarkable situations.

She started her career as a painter and fashion model, before drifting into acting. Kendall scored a minor role in *The Liquidator,* a 1965 spy thriller starring Rod Taylor and Jill St. John, and had an uncredited bit-part in the 1965 Bond hit *Thunderball.* She had a more prominent part in the 1966 horror film *Circus of Fear* with Christopher Lee, but it was *To Sir, With Love* the following year that gave her the best exposure to date, playing a sexy teacher working alongside Sidney Poitier in a seedy London school. The film proved a massive hit. Kendall followed it with Peter Collinson's kinky sex thriller *The Penthouse* (1967), and less than 18 months after entering show business the press had named her 'one of Britain's most sought-after young actresses'.

In 1967 she secured her biggest role, again working with Collinson, in *Up the Junction,* a big screen version of the controversial BBC TV play which had addressed some of the day's major social issues. That same year she married popular actor/musician/comedian Dudley Moore and the two co-starred in the 1968 comedy *30 is a Dangerous Age, Cynthia.* The couple divorced in 1972, but remained close friends. (Kendall, who had married again, eulogised Moore at his funeral in 2002.)

After the poorly received *Fraulein Doktor* (1969), where she played the title role of a female spy in the First World War, Kendall appeared in two 1970 cult hits. She reunited with Rod Taylor for the crime thriller *Darker Than Amber* and also starred in director Dario

Argento's classic slasher flick *The Bird With the Crystal Plumage.* Following a leading role in the Alistair MacLean thriller *Fear is the Key* (1972), work on the big screen became more infrequent. Kendall therefore turned to B movies and British TV shows like *The Persuaders!* and *Van der Valk.*

She authored a book about beauty treatments in 1980, but has since lived relatively quietly with her second husband in London. Her last credited screen appearance was in 1977.

Top: *Up the Junction.*
Below: *Darker Than Amber* with Rod Taylor.
Opposite: On-location cheesecake pose during the making of *Darker Than Amber.*

VALERIE LEON

Leon learned early on in her career that her remarkable figure and ample bust could be major assets. She went on to earn appearances in some of the touchstones of seventies British popular cinema: James Bond, Hammer, *Carry On*, British sex comedies, *The Pink Panther* and, on the small screen, the Hai Karate adverts.

Born in England in 1943, Valerie Leon aspired to be an actress from an early age but was turned down by RADA. Undaunted, she played 'hooky' from her day job at Harrods as a fashion buyer and successfully auditioned for the chorus in the play *The Belle of New York*. The play was a flop, but Leon was hooked on acting and she soon had a supporting role in the London production of *Funny Girl* with Barbra Streisand.

Guest starring roles in the TV series *The Saint*, *The Baron* and *The Avengers* followed. Her breakthrough was her appearance as a sexy femme fatale in the Hai Karate aftershave TV ads that afforded her international prominence. The campaign ran between 1969 and 1975 and certainly helped her gain some substantial film roles.

Producer Peter Rogers became a fan and hired Leon to appear in several of the *Carry On* series. She began to alternate bit roles in high-quality productions like *The Italian Job* (1969) with larger parts in popular British sex comedies, among them *No Sex, Please: We're British* (1973) and *Can You Keep It Up for a Week?* (1974). In the 1971 Hammer film, *Blood From the Mummy's Tomb*, Leon had the starring role and featured prominently in publicity photos, scantily-clad in ancient Egyptian attire. The film retains a loyal cult following to this day. Leon's career could have progressed even further, but despite capitalising on her physical beauty she refused to appear topless on screen.

In 1977 she had a bit role in Roger Moore's James Bond hit *The Spy Who Loved Me*, and the following year made another small but memorable appearance as a dominatrix in *Revenge of the Pink Panther*, as well as taking a part in the hit adventure film *The Wild Geese*. In 1983 there was a prominent role as one of James Bond's bedmates in the 007 film *Never Say Never Again*, which starred Sean Connery in a remake of his earlier movie *Thunderball* (1965). Leon plays a vivacious woman who literally fishes James Bond out of the ocean and narrowly escapes being blown to pieces when she becomes his one-night stand.

Leon continues to act today, appearing in British stage productions, commercials and taking guest spots on popular TV series like *The Last of the Summer Wine*. She has also created a one-woman show about her life and career that she periodically performs throughout Europe. Leon keeps in touch with her fans through her website and regularly attends autograph fairs. She has also published a booklet about her experiences in show business. The title, appropriately enough, is *Everything But the Nipple*.

Top: *Carry On Again Doctor* (1969).
Below: Appearing in six films in the series, Valerie's role as Leda in *Carry On Up the Jungle* (1970) was the most outstanding of them all.
Opposite: The dual parts of Margaret Fuchs and Queen Tera in Hammer's *Blood From the Mummy's Tomb* provided Valerie with what many consider her most memorable screen appearance.

HELEN MIRREN

One of the great British stage and screen actresses, Helen Mirren was born Ilyena Lydia Mironoff in London in 1945. She has since conquered stage, cinema and the small screen, giving a string of powerful performances in every medium she's turned her hand to.

The daughter of a Russian father and British mother, Mirren began acting in school plays and later attended the New College of Speech and Drama in London before being accepted in the National Youth Theatre. Her rise was meteoric. At the tender age of 20, she was performing Shakespeare at the Old Vic. Mirren later joined the Royal Shakespeare Company and starred in numerous international productions directed by Trevor Nunn. High-profile stage roles followed over the years and she gained widespread acclaim for her performance in the 1994 production of *A Month in the Country*. Since then, Mirren's appearances on stage have been major events, virtually guaranteeing a show's financial success.

Mirren made her screen début in 1966 but gained little attention until she starred opposite James Mason in Michael Powell's 1969 May/December romance *Age of Consent*. It was in this film that Mirren first demonstrated her ease at appearing nude on screen. Stardom did not follow immediately, despite appearances in Ken Russell's *Savage Messiah* (1972), Lindsay Anderson's *O Lucky Man!* (1973) and the notorious *Penthouse* production of *Caligula* (1979).

Throughout the Eighties she worked consistently in films of varying quality. Highlights include the classic British gangster

film *The Long Good Friday* (1980), *Excalibur* (1981), *Cal* (1984) and Peter Weir's underrated *The Mosquito Coast* (1986) opposite Harrison Ford. As Mirren's stature rose in the theatre world, she was able to chose her film projects with increasing care, often electing to appear in arthouse films with limited commercial appeal. Among her more high-profile movies are *The Cook, the Thief, His Wife & Her Lover* (1989), *The Comfort of Strangers* (1990), *The Madness of King George* (1994) and *Calendar Girls* (2003).

One of her most important roles was undoubtedly as HRH Queen Elizabeth in *The Queen* (2006), portraying the person who had awarded her the title of Dame Commander of the Order of the British Empire (DBE) in 2003. Mirren's superb performance earned her an Oscar, a BAFTA, a Golden Globe and numerous other awards.

Mirren has conquered every medium in which she has performed. Her starring role in the 1990s British TV detective show *Prime Suspect* attracted large audiences and won her an Emmy. After a long romance with director Taylor Hackford, the couple wed in 1997.

Mirren, who says she has no maternal instincts, has no children of her own. In 2007, she published her autobiography, *My Life in Words and Pictures*. Outspoken, witty and refreshingly candid, Mirren continues to explore new horizons, whilst her stature as one of the most acclaimed actresses of her generation grows each year.

Top: *Age of Consent*.
Above: British quad poster for *Hussy* (1980).
Left: Helen Mirren in Peter Greenaway's arthouse hit *The Cook, the Thief, His Wife and Her Lover*.

CAROLINE MUNRO

Born in England in 1949, Caroline Munro originally studied art in the hope of pursuing a career as an artist. However, at the same time Munro's mother entered her photograph in a David Bailey contest to find the Face of the Year. She emerged a winner and within a short time was on the road to a successful modeling and acting career, with roles for Hammer and in a James Bond movie to follow.

Munro then took the opportunity to dabble in acting and, at the tender age of 16, had an uncredited part as one of Woody Allen's sexy female agents in the 1967 James Bond spoof *Casino Royale*. Just as her acting career was starting to take off, Munro signed a contract to be the model for Lamb's Navy Rum in 1969. Over a ten-year period, Munro's scantily-clad image adorned adverts and billboards for the product all over the UK.

Although she considered modeling her main career, she was cast in the prominent role of Richard Widmark's daughter in the Paramount film *A Talent for Loving* (1969). Munro was the only actress signed to a long-term contract by Hammer Films, although this only resulted in her making two movies for the studio: *Dracula A.D. 1972* (1972) with Christopher Lee and

Captain Kronos, Vampire Hunter (1974). Her aversion to appearing nude on screen led to the dissolution of the contract.

She also appeared in a small but memorable role opposite Vincent Price in *The Abominable Dr. Phibes* (1971) and its 1972 sequel, *Dr. Phibes Rises Again*. *Captain Kronos* director Brian Clemens, who championed her career, fought to get Munro the female lead in the 1974 Ray Harryhausen film *The Golden Voyage of Sinbad*, and she also starred with Peter Cushing and Doug McClure in the hit 1976 sci-fi adventure *At the Earth's Core*.

In 1977, Munro gained even more fame with her role as the evil, seductive spy Naomi in the James Bond movie *The Spy Who Loved Me* opposite Roger Moore. She rounded off the decade with another prominent part, this time

in director William Lustig's cult classic *Maniac* (1980).

However, Munro was beginning to concentrate more on raising her children, although she would occasionally act in low-budget movies like cult favourite *Starcrash* (1979) and Jess Franco's *Faceless* (1987). She still occasionally acts and is a regular at international autograph fairs. Munro's affable personality and willingness to engage with her fans ensures her status as one of the most popular presences at these events.

Top: *Starcrash.*
Below left and opposite: As the beautiful but doomed Laura Bellows in *Dracula A.D. 1972.*
Below right: As Margiana opposite John Phillip Law in Ray Harryhausen's *The Golden Voyage of Sinbad.*

INGRID PITT

Ingrid Pitt was born Ingoushka Petrov (though by some accounts her birth name was Irena Wassiljewna Petronowitscht) in Poland in 1937. The exotically named beauty used her spectacular looks to become Hammer's reigning scream queen during the early Seventies.

As a young woman, Pitt lived in Berlin and took up acting, becoming a member of the Berliner Ensemble Theatre Company run by Bertolt Brecht's widow. However, she was miserable living under yet another totalitarian regime and spoke out against the communist authorities. Learning she was to be arrested, Pitt orchestrated a dramatic escape to the West.

Pitt married an American military man who had helped her escape and, for a period, lived with him in Colorado. They had one daughter, Steffanie, who is now an actress. Following her divorce, Pitt moved to Spain, where she landed small parts in *Doctor Zhivago* (1965), *Chimes at Midnight* (1966) and *A Funny Thing Happened on the Way to the Forum* (1966). She was uncredited in all of these major films, but had a supporting role in the Spanish film *Sound of Horror* (1966).

Pitt found better luck in England, when she was cast in a key role in the 1968 MGM Second World War epic *Where Eagles Dare*, starring Richard Burton and Clint Eastwood. She played a seemingly innocent young woman who is actually an undercover agent for Allied Intelligence. Her perky personality and ample bosom were used to promote the picture and led to work in other British films.

When Hammer came calling, Pitt agreed to doff her clothes and play a lesbian vampire in *The Vampire Lovers* (1970). As she recalled in her autobiography, *Life's A Scream*: "The film involved nude scenes. I'd never done the full frontal bit before but I was proud of my body and not too reluctant to show it. I soon discovered that when you're naked on set everyone is terribly nice to you and looks after you beyond the call of duty. This is particularly the case when you're doing a bath scene, which I seemed to do a lot of at Hammer."

The film was a major hit and within short order Pitt was starring in Hammer's *Countess Dracula* (1970). She followed this by playing another vampire, this time in Amicus' portmanteau film *The House That Dripped Blood* (1970), as well as appearing in a supporting role in the 1973 cult classic *The Wicker Man*. However, Pitt never became a box-office draw outside horror movies, although she did find a good role in the thriller *Who Dares Wins* (1982, aka *The Final Option*) and appeared in a number of popular TV shows, including *Doctor Who*.

Despite a relatively thin résumé, Pitt established a loyal and enthusiastic fan base. She mastered the art of self-marketing, appearing at countless international film fairs, horror movie screenings and autograph shows with her husband, former race car driver Tony Rudlin. Pitt was the author of a number of books and in 1999 wrote her autobiography, titled *Life's a Scream*. She died in 2010 in London whilst on her way to a celebration of her career being held by her fans.

Opposite: No man – or woman – could resist the charms of the Karnstein lovely in Hammer's classic lesbian vampire opus *The Vampire Lovers*.
Top: *The Wicker Man.*
Above: On location with Richard Burton in Austria during the filming of *Where Eagles Dare.*

MADELiNE SMiTH

Coming of age in the 1960s during a more relaxed era of film censorship, Madeline Smith found a ready audience for her innocent demeanour and spectacular figure. She was born in England in 1949 and started her career as a model, before landing bit roles that emphasised her physical assets.

She was quoted as saying: "I was a late developer in every sense. At 21, I became interested in men for the first time and men became more interested in me. My body reacted by producing this enormous bosom. It had nothing to do with the Pill, which I've never taken." This was not entirely due to nature. Smith had wanted a more voluptuous chest to enhance her career. Writing in *Cinema Retro* in 2005, she recalled: "In the winter of 1969, I came across muesli yoghurt. I ate so much that if my breasts were to be dissected today, they would find them made only of breakfast cereal! Within a month my bosoms flowered. The rest of my body couldn't keep up, however. My doll-like arms bore witness to this over-hasty dairy-fest."

Not surprisingly, she found a welcome reception in the film industry, although she was relegated to cinematic eye candy in the likes of *Some Like it Sexy* (1969) until Hammer Films

came calling. Smith landed a role in the 1969 production *Taste the Blood of Dracula* starring Christopher Lee. Suitably impressed, Hammer immediately hired her to appear with Ingrid Pitt in the lesbian-themed *The Vampire Lovers* (1970) and Smith endeared herself to male cinemagoers for decades to come for the sequence in which Pitt disrobes and seduces her.

In 1971, she won a prominent role in the British sex farce *Up Pompeii* starring Frankie Howerd. Amidst other undistinguished comedies of the era, she also appeared in *Carry on Matron* (1972). The following year, she became a Bond Girl in *Live and Let Die*, featuring as a seductive Italian agent in the first scene of Roger Moore's début film as 007. Smith also appeared in two cult horror films around this time, taking a small role in the macabre Vincent Price comedy *Theatre of Blood* and returning to Hammer in 1973 for *Frankenstein and the Monster From Hell*.

During the 1970s, she also made guest appearances on popular TV series such as *Steptoe and Son, The Persuaders!, The Two Ronnies, Jason King* and *Clochemerle*. By the mid-Eighties Smith had largely retired from acting, having married actor David Buck and decided it would be best to spend her time raising their daughter. She remained married to Buck until his death in 1989. Today, Smith enjoys a loyal fan following and is a frequent guest at autograph shows in the UK.

Opposite: As Erotica, trying to hide her more than ample bust in a saucy publicity pose for the big-screen version of the hit TV show, *Up Pompeii*.
Top: *Frankenstein and the Monster From Hell.*
Below: About to be seduced by Carmilla (Ingrid Pitt) in *The Vampire Lovers.*

BRiT GLAMOUR ROUND-UP

No tribute to sex sirens can overlook the distinguished ladies who, whilst never quite becoming box-office stars, were regulars on British television and cinema screens. And all of the following actresses added glamour to the popular Hammer horrors of the Sixties and Seventies.

Probably the best-known is Martine Beswick, the Jamaican-born actress who also appeared in the 007 movies *From Russia With Love* (1963) and *Thunderball* (1965). Among those taking note was Hammer Films producer James Carreras, who gave Beswick a key part in *One Million Years B.C.* (1966), followed by the lead in their prehistoric follow-up *Slave Girls* (1967, aka *Prehistoric Women*). Beswick's best role came in Hammer's *Dr. Jekyll & Sister Hyde* (1971), as one half of the title role opposite Ralph Bates' Hyde, providing both chills and sexual thrills in a finely crafted performance.

In the Seventies, Beswick (who is sometimes credited as 'Beswicke') made guest appearances in many top American TV series. On the big screen, however, her talents were under-utilised and she was mostly relegated to sexploitation films like *The Last Italian Tango* (1973) and *The Happy Hooker Goes Hollywood* (1980).

She found a rare interesting role in Oliver Stone's directorial début, playing The Queen of Evil in *Seizure* (1974). Beswick last worked in films in the mid-Nineties and has since established her own business in London. However, she still proves to be a popular presence at international movie fairs, where Beswick signs autographs for her legions of loyal fans.

If any actress lives up to the designation sex siren, it is Linda Hayden, who made a memorable screen début in the controversial British film *Baby Love* (1968), playing a seductive and scheming 15 year old who uses her sexuality to divide a family. Much publicity was generated by the fact that she wasn't even old enough to see the film, since it was granted an 'X' certificate (meaning no one under 16 would be admitted). Born in 1953, the beautiful actress was immediately sought by Hammer,

who gave her the female lead in *Taste the Blood of Dracula* (1969). A year later Hayden had what is probably her best role, in the cult-classic *Blood on Satan's Claw* (aka *Satan's Skin*).

Over the next few years she appeared a succession of TV shows, and in 1974 starred in the films *Vampira*, *Confessions of a Window Cleaner* and *Madhouse*. However, the ultra-violent and sexually explicit *Exposé* (1975) and the unreleased *Queen Kong* (1976) were both definite career low-points. These roles were followed by *Confessions From a Holiday Camp* (1977), *Let's Get Laid* (1978) and a minor part in *The Boys From Brazil* (1978), the latter requiring her to be naked, a common component of her films during this period. Hayden returned to films in 2009 to appear in a remake of *Exposé*, this time playing the mother of the character she originally portrayed.

Opposite top: Julie Ege in *Every Home Should Have One*.
Opposite below: Could you resist the advances of Queen Kari? Martine Beswick in *Slave Girls*.
Top left: The beautiful but deadly Sister Hyde in Roy Ward Baker's brilliant Hammer horror, *Dr Jekyll & Sister Hyde*.
Above left: Hammer glamour. Martine Beswick, looking as gorgeous as ever.
Above: Falling victim to the count. Linda Hayden in *Taste the Blood of Dracula*.
Left: Linda Hayden as a scheming teenager, who uses her sexual prowess to destroy a family in *Baby Love*.

Scandanavian-born actress Julie Ege is best known for her appearances in British films. Originally a model, winning both Miss Norway and Miss Universe, an appearance as a 'Penthouse Pet' in the famed men's magazine brought her to the UK. Her acting début came with an uncredited appearance in Peter Yates' *Robbery* (1967), which led to a small part in the James Bond film *On Her Majesty's Secret Service* (1969). However, it wasn't until Ege played Inga in *Every Home Should Have One* (1970) that the world took notice. Stunningly beautiful, with a perfect figure, she appeared in over 15 films within the next five years, including *Up Pompeii* (1971), *Creatures the World Forgot* (1971), *The Legend of the 7 Golden Vampires* (1974), and *Percy's Progress* (1974), to name but a few.

In 1976 Ege returned to her native Norway, but made just one film and a TV mini-series in 1988 and 1998 respectively. During this period, she fulfilled a life-time's dream by gaining a licence to work as a registered nurse, helping the afflicted at a hospital in Oslo. Sadly, Ege was diagnosed with both breast and lung cancer. She bravely soldiered on with her nursing duties before succumbing to the disease in 2008 at age 64.

Stephanie Beacham was another actress unashamed to flaunt her bodily charms. Her career started in modeling (including full frontal nudity), after which she played minor roles in TV shows like *The Saint*, *Callan* and *UFO*. She also appeared nude in an early film role, having a steamy sex scene with Marlon Brando in Michael Winner's S&M-themed *The Nightcomers* (1971). Beacham was then signed by Hammer Films to appear in *Dracula A.D. 1972* alongside Caroline Munro, wearing a series of skimpy dresses that hardly concealed her more-than-ample bust.

The majority of work that followed was for television, although she had substantial parts in *…And Now the Screaming Starts!* (1973) and a series of low-budget horror flicks made by cult director Pete Walker: *House of Mortal Sin* (1975), *Schizo* (1976) and *Inseminoid* (1981). In the Eighties she starred in both *The Colby's* and *Dynasty*, as well as other well-known American shows like *Star Trek: The Next Generation*. Now living back in England, Beacham continues to work regularly on mainstream television shows, including the long-running soap opera *Coronation Street*.

The Collinson Twins were models Mary and Madeleine Collinson. The identical twins, born in Malta in 1952, moved to England in 1969. Shortly after their arrival in the UK, photographer and filmmaker Harrison Marks, who specialised in eroticism, cast them in a sexploitation film, *Halfway Inn*, which was made specifically for the 8mm collector's market. Donovan Winter next featured them in his sex comedy *Some Like it Sexy (1969)*, which also featured a young Madeline Smith.

Before long, the sisters had caught the eye of *Playboy* titan Hugh Hefner, who gave them a sensational showcase as Playmates of the Month in October 1970. Over the next two years the girls appeared in *Permissive* (1970), *Groupie Girl* (1970), *She'll Follow You Anywhere* (1971) and *The Love Machine* (1971). Always looking for a 'new angle', Hammer fashioned *Twins of Evil* (1971) especially for the Collinsons, although both of the sister's voices were dubbed. After less than two years in the business, Mary and Madeleine quit the industry at the age of 19, opting instead to live 'normal' lives.

Opposite: It's easy to work out why Julie Ege, seen here as Voluptua in *Up Pompeii*, soon found herself inundated with work after arriving in Britain from her native Norway.

Top left: Julie Ege.

Top right: Nobody could tell the difference between Mary and Madeleine Collinson during the filming of *Twins of Evil*.

Above right: The Collinson Twins, seen here with John Phillip Law in a scene from *The Love Machine*, on the cover of *Cinema X*.

Left: Stephanie Beacham's steamy love scene with Marlon Brando in *The Nightcomers* was fairly explicit. This publicity still was issued with Ms Beacham's pubic hair airbrushed out!

Yvonne Romain personifies the word 'glamour', oozing sex appeal and sensuality in every frame of film. Her career wasn't a long one, although this was due to her own decision rather than indicating any lack of popularity. Born Yvonne Warren in the late Thirties (her parents were of Maltese and British descent), she studied at the Italia Conti Academy in London and was a child actor from the age of 12. By her late teens Romain had developed a 38-22-36 figure and was soon in demand by film producers, both for her stunning figure and her dark exotic features.

She was considered ideal for roles as European girls and her first film part was playing an Italian girl in *The Baby and the Battleship* (1956). Romain acted alongside Sean Connery in *Action of the Tiger* (1957) and *The Frightened City* (1961), the latter seeing her share equal billing with the soon-to-be Bond star. Roles in the horror films *Corridors of Blood* (1958) and *Circus of Horrors* (1960) brought her to the attention of Hammer Films,

for whom she made three films: *The Curse of the Werewolf* (1961), *Captain Clegg* (1962) and *The Brigand of Kandahar* (1965). The publicity department went overboard in taking advantage of Romain's ample bust, which, more often than not, was displayed in the lowest-cut tops deemed acceptable to the censor.

During this ten-year period she also worked on many many popular British television shows, including *The Buccaneers, Interpol, Armchair Theatre* and *Danger Man*, to name but a few. Following her marriage to famed composer Leslie Bricusse, she moved to America in the mid-Sixties and appeared in the Ann-Margret film *The Swinger* (1966) and with Elvis Presley in *Double Trouble* (1967). Romain retired shortly afterwards to start a family, but made a small comeback in 1973 to play the titular role in the star-packed murder mystery *The Last of Sheila,* although she also turned down a long-term contract with Fellini for fear it would keep her away from her family for too long. Both Romain and her husband now reside in London.

Veronica Carlson's short-lived career took in several British films of the Sixties and has earned her a dedicated following among horror-film aficionados, particularly for her roles in Hammer's *Dracula Has Risen From the Grave* (1968), *Frankenstein Must Be Destroyed* (1969) and *The Horror of Frankenstein* (1970). Although she was frequently cast in 'innocent' roles, the publicity machine worked overtime releasing specially posed, scantily clad images of Carlson.

Born in England, the actress was first seen in bit-part roles in films like *The Magnificent Two* and *Smashing Time*, both released in 1967, as well as in celebrated TV shows such as *The Saint* and *Department S.* Carlson also appeared in Roger Moore's *Crossplot* (1969), *Pussycat, Pussycat, I Love You* (1970), *Vampira* (1974) and *The Ghoul* (1975). Like many of the era's actresses, Carlson put her career on the back-burner when she married and had a family. Today, she is an acclaimed artist living in Florida and is often commissioned to create artwork based on the Hammer movies, which she still regards with great affection.

Opposite top and bottom: The stunning and incredibly sexy Yvonne Romain, both in and out of costume, promoting the Hammer film *The Brigand of Kandahar*.
This page: Veronica Carlson became the object of Count Dracula's desires in *Dracula Has Risen From the Grave*.

Following a convent education, Suzanna Leigh entered the world of show business aged just 13, an early role coming as a dancer in the MGM production *Tom Thumb* (1958). Born Suzanna Smyth, she took the stage name Leigh after admiring actress Vivien Leigh and as a teenager had bit parts in TV shows such as *The Saint* and films like *Oscar Wilde* (1960) and *The Pleasure Girls* (1965). At age 20, movie producer Hal B. Wallis saw her publicity photographs and Leigh was whisked off to Hollywood to appear in *Boeing Boeing* (1965), with stars Jerry Lewis and Tony Curtis, and *Paradise, Hawaiian Style* (1966), opposite Elvis Presley.

Returning to England, she took the lead role in *The Deadly Bees* (1966) and was also cast in *Deadlier Than the Male* (1967) alongside Richard Johnson, Sylva Koscina and Elke Sommer. Not surprisingly, Hammer knocked on her door with the offer of a lead role in *The Lost Continent* (1968), and later *Lust for a Vampire* (1971). In 1971, Leigh also appeared in an episode of the TV show *The Persuaders!* with Tony Curtis and Roger Moore. She last worked in films in 1974, appearing in the disastrous *Son of Dracula*, and now lives in Memphis with her daughter. Due to her

association with Elvis, Leigh often appears at nearby Graceland for Presley tributes. In 1998 she wrote her autobiography *Paradise, Suzanna Style.*

Born in England in 1948, Judy Geeson, older sister of actress Sally Geeson, blossomed in the Sixties through appearances on popular TV series like *The Newcomers* and *Danger Man.* Her first major break came with a starring role in the mod sex comedy *Here We Go 'Round the Mulberry Bush* (1967). That same year, she gained favourable notices for her performance as a wayward schoolgirl in the smash hit film *To Sir, With Love* opposite Sidney Poitier. Although Geeson never became a major 'name-above-the-title' star, her drawing power at the box office earnt her prominent roles alongside major names in films like *Berserk!* (1967, with Joan Crawford), *Prudence and the Pill* (1968, with Deborah Kerr and David Niven), *Three Into Two Won't Go* (1969, with Rod Steiger) and *10 Rillington Place* (1970, with Richard Attenborough).

Geeson was also the female lead in two spy movies during this period: *Hammerhead* (1968), alongside Vince Edwards, and *The Executioner* (1970), opposite George Peppard. Then there was a memorable performance in the 1970 film

Goodbye, Gemini, a creepy concoction in which she starred with Martin Potter as possibly incestuous twins who dabble in murderous activities. In 1972, Geeson appeared in the Hammer film *Fear in the Night* with Peter Cushing and Joan Collins and Tigon's *Doomwatch,* whilst three years later she played a sexy but tough Scotland Yard detective in the hit John Wayne thriller *Brannigan* (1975).

As the Seventies came to a close, the major film roles began to evaporate, though Geeson continued to act. She was seen in the 1976 comedy *Carry on England,* had a supporting role in the big-budget war film *The Eagle Has Landed* (1976) and played the lead in Pete Walker's *Inseminoid* (1981). She had far more success on television, however, starring in the popular series *Poldark* and *Danger UXB,* among others.

Since then, Geeson has appeared regularly on top shows in the UK and America, including recurring roles in the sitcoms *Mad About You* and *The Gilmore Girls.* She was married in the Eighties to actor Kristoffer Tabori, but the couple divorced in 1989. More recently, she owned an antique store in Beverly Hills.

Opposite: Hammer regular Suzanna Leigh poses for a photograph on the grounds of Hazelwood House during the filming of *Lust for a Vampire*.
Above left and left: Judy Geeson and Barry Evans played the starry-eyed lovers in the teen comedy *Here We Go 'Round the Mulberry Bush*.
Top right: Known as 'The Countess of Cleavage', it's not surprising that busty model Imogen Hassall found herself appearing scantily-clad in Hammer's dinosaur flick *When Dinosaurs Ruled the Earth* (1970).
Above right: Luan Peters, seen here in Pete Walker's *Man of Violence* (1970), was a popular choice with producers of horror films or saucy comedies during the Seventies.

SEX SELLS:
THE ART OF THE MOVIE POSTER

"A picture is worth a thousand words." Or in the case of movie marketing, millions at the box office. The movie poster has always been one of the key elements when it comes to selling films. Once dismissed as disposable, some of these posters have become expensive, much-sought-after collector's items which today turn up in leading auction houses.

Sex was always used to sell movies, even prestigious studio fare. Major productions frequently used sexual imagery in less-than-subliminal ways to entice audiences. Whether the art played up Jane Russell's bosom for *The Outlaw* (1943) (one of the film's posters bore the memorable tag-line: 'TWO Great NEW DISCOVERIES!'), Dean Martin riding a phallic pistol for *The Silencers* (1966) or James Bond seen through the open legs of a bikini-clad woman in the campaign for *For Your Eyes Only* (1981), eroticism is obviously woven into the very fabric of movie publicity. This is even more blatant when it comes to pure sexploitation films, where the prurient content has frequently been conveyed in a no-holds-barred fashion through a striking image or tag-line. This has resulted in direct, in-your-face campaigns that have left little doubt as to what the producers were really selling.

That's not to diminish the artistry that went into the creation of many of these posters. In fact many artists, such as Tom Chantrell, Reynolds Brown and Robert McGinnis, are now avidly collected by fans. From prestigious major studio releases to low-rent exploitation films, enjoy these glorious examples from the golden age of movie marketing.

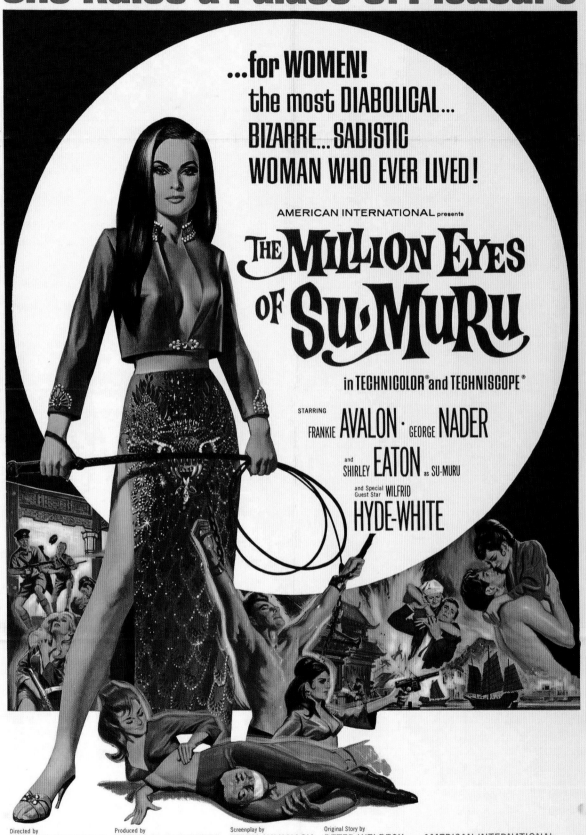

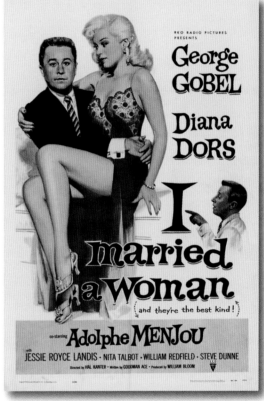

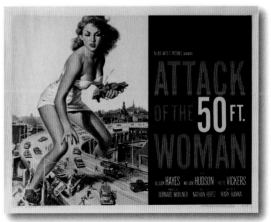

"THIS IS THE FIRST TIME I'VE EVER APPEARED COMPLETELY NUDE!"
JAYNE MANSFIELD in PLAYBOY MAGAZINE

"Promises! Promises!"

UNCUT!
UNCENSORED!
EUROPEAN VERSION!

starring

JAYNE MANSFIELD · MARIE McDONALD · TOMMY NOONAN

A NOONAN-TAYLOR Production   Released by NTD, Inc.

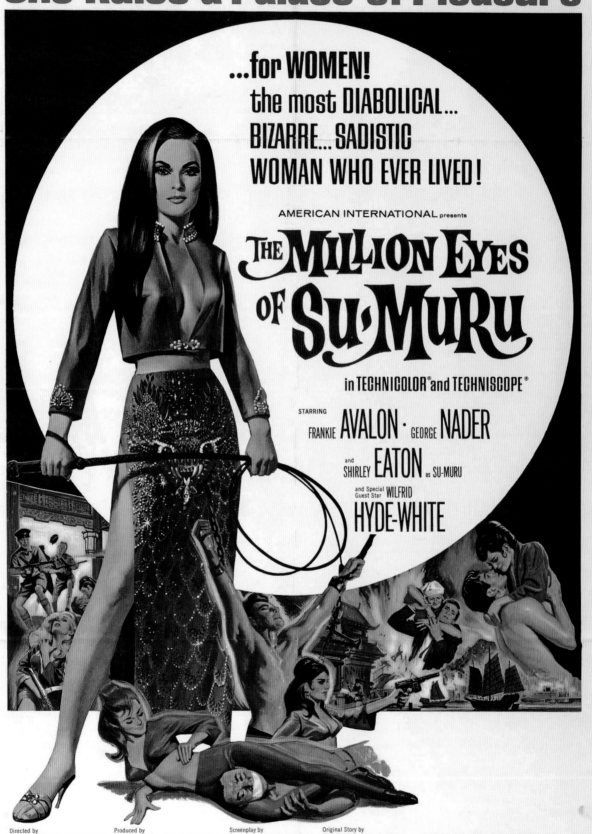

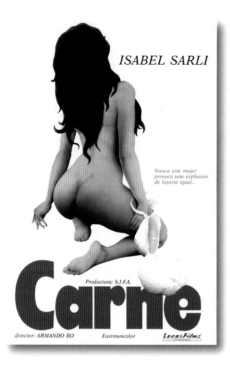

ISABEL SARLI

Nunca una mujer
provocó una explosión
de lujuria igual...

Carne

Productora: S.I.F.A.

director: ARMANDO BO   Eastmancolor   LecasFilms

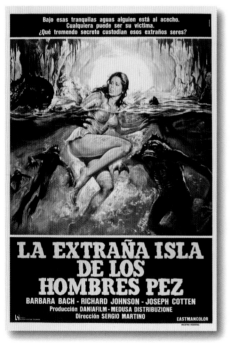

Bajo esas tranquilas aguas alguien está al acecho.
Cualquiera puede ser su víctima.
¿Qué tremendo secreto custodian esos extraños seres?

**LA EXTRAÑA ISLA
DE LOS
HOMBRES PEZ**

BARBARA BACH · RICHARD JOHNSON · JOSEPH COTTEN
Producción DANIAFILM - MEDUSA DISTRIBUZIONE
Dirección SERGIO MARTINO   EASTMANCOLOR

Les Films *Jacques Leitienne* présentent

EDWIGE FENECH ★ RENZO MONTAGNANI
dans

**la "Prof"
et les
Cancres**

avec **ALVARO VITALI ★ LEO COLONNA ★ NIKI GENTILE**
CARLO SPOSITO ★ avec **LUCIO MONTANARO** ★ et avec **LINO BANFI**
et avec la participation de **GIANFRANCO D'ANGELO** mise en scène de **MARIANO LAURENTI**
une coproduction italo française
DEVON FILM · MEDUSA DISTRIBUTION - **LES FILMS JACQUES LEITIENNE · IMP.EX.CI.** · **EASTMANCOLOR**

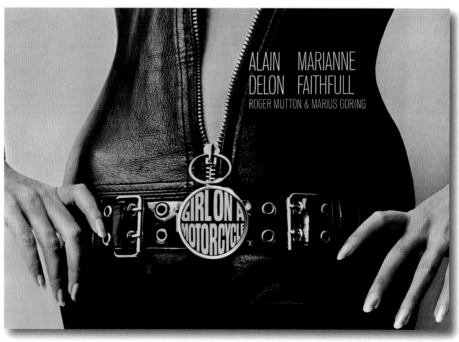

ALAIN   MARIANNE
DELON   FAITHFULL
ROGER MUTTON & MARIUS GORING

GIRL ON A
MOTORCYCLE
X

BIBLIOGRAPHY

Books
Fantasy Females. (edited by Allan Bryce; Stray Cat Publishing, 2000)
Life's a Scream (Ingrid Pitt; William Heinemann/Random House, 1999)
A Pictorial History of Sex in the Movies (Jeremy Pascall & Clyde Jeavons; Hamlyn Publishing Group, 1975)
Sophia: Living and Loving. Her Own Story (Sophia Loren; Michael Joseph Limited, 1979)
The Very Breast of Russ Meyer (edited by Paul A. Woods; Plexus Publishing Ltd, 2004)
Winner Takes All: A Life of Sorts (Michael Winner; Robson Books, 2004)

Magazines
Cinema Retro, September 2005 (Cinema Retro Inc)
Cinema Retro, January 2008 (Cinema Retro Inc)
Cinema Retro, May 2010 (Cinema Retro Inc)
The Daily Mail, September17th, 2010
The Telegraph, August 20th, 2009

And if you want to know more about your favourite cinema sex sirens, we'd like to suggest you check out the following websites and publications from the ladies themselves!

Ann-Margret
Ann-Margret: My Story (Putnam Adult, 1994)
www.ann-margret.com

Carroll Baker
Baby Doll: An Autobiography (Arbor House Pub Co, 1983)

Brigitte Bardot
Initiales B.B.: Memoires (Grasset and Fasquelle, 1995)

Stephanie Beacham
Many Lives (Hay House UK, 2011)
www.simplystephaniebeacham.com

Senta Berger
I Knew That I Could Fly (Kein & Aber, 2006)

Jane Birkin
www.janebirkin.net

Claudia Cardinale
Moi, Claudia, Toi, Claudia La Roman d'une Vie (Grasset, 1995)
Mes Etoiles (Michel Lafon, 2004)

Joan Collins
Past Imperfect (W.H. Allen, 1978)
Second Act: An Autobiography (Boxtree, 1996)
www.joancollins.net

Sybil Danning
www.sybildanning.net

Diana Dors
Behind Closed Dors (Star, 1979)
www.dianadors.co.uk

Shirley Eaton
Golden Girl (B.T. Batsford, 2000)
www.shirleyeaton.net

Julie Ege
Naken (H. Aschenhoug & Co, 2002)

Britt Ekland
True Britt (Sphere, 1980)
www.brittekland.com

Shirley Anne Field
A Time for Love (Bantam, 1991)

Jane Fonda
My Life So Far (Random Press, 2005)
www.janefonda.com

Susan George
www.susangeorgeofficialwebsite.com

Pam Grier
Foxy: My Life in Three Acts (Springboard Press, 2010)

Gloria Hendry
Gloria (Xlibris Corporation, 2008)
www.gloriahendry.com

Sylvia Kristel
Undressing Emmanuelle: A Memoir (Fourth Estate, 2007)

Daliah Lavi
www.daliah-lavi.com

Janet Leigh
There Really Was a Hollywood (Doubleday, 1984)

Suzanna Leigh
Paradise, Suzanna Style (Pen Press Publishers, 1998)

Valerie Leon
In the Leon's Den (self-published)
www.valerieleon.com

Gina Lollobrigida
www.ginalollobrigida.com

Sophia Loren
Sophia: Living and Loving. Her Own Story (Michael Joseph Limited, 1979)

Jayne Mansfield
www.jaynemansfield.com

Marisa Mell
Coverlove (Graz, 1990)

Helen Mirren
In the Frame: My Life in Words and Pictures (Weidenfeld & Nicholson, 2007)
www.helenmirrenofficial.com

Caroline Munro
www.carolinemunro.org

Margaret Nolan
www.margaretnolan.co.uk

Kate O'Mara
Game Plan: A Modern Woman's Survival Kit (Sedgwick & Jackson, 1990)
Vamp Until Ready (Robson Books, 2003)

Luciana Paluzzi
www.lucianapaluzzi.com/

Ingrid Pitt
Life's a Scream (William Heinemann/Random House, 1999)
Darkness Before Dawn (Midnight Marquee Press, 2008, revised and expanded edition of *Life's a Scream*)
www.pittofhorror.com

Jane Russell
My Path and My Detours (Franklin Watts, 1985)

Tura Satana
www.turasatana.com

Stella Stevens
www.stellastevens.biz

Sylvia Syms
www.sylviasyms.co.uk

Sharon Tate
www.sharontate.net

Mamie Van Doren
Playing the Field (G.P. Putnam, 1987)
www.mamievandoren.com

Raquel Welch
Raquel: Beyond the Cleavage (Weinstein Books, 2010)

Natalie Wood
www.cmgww.com/stars/wood

About the Authors

Dave Worrall is a graphic designer by trade and the co-publisher (with Lee Pfeiffer) of *Cinema Retro* magazine, which is dedicated to films of the 1960s and 1970s. The magazine's web site at www.cinemaretro.com attracts hundreds of thousands of movie fans each month. Worrall established the highly successful company Solo Publishing in 1987, which has produced high profile magazines and books pertaining to the James Bond phenomenon. He has also discussed cinema on countless British and American radio and TV programmes and was the UK Field Producer on most of the James Bond DVD documentaries for MGM Home Entertainment. Worrall is also the author of *The Most Famous Car in the World*, the definitive history of the

cinema at New York University and co-wrote and produced DVD documentaries about the James Bond films for MGM and the career of Stanley Kubrick for Sony. A native American, he resides in New Jersey but can't resist frequent visits to England where he runs film location trips through his company T.W.I.N.E Tours.

Acknowledgements:

The authors would also like to express their thanks to Sir Roger Moore for graciously providing the foreword and reflecting on working with some of the legendary ladies celebrated in this book. For years, Sir Roger has proven to be a good friend and supporter of *Cinema Retro*'s projects and we thank him for his time and consideration.

Photo credits

The majority of the advertising material and photographs that appear in this book come from the following picture libraries and the archive of Cinema Retro Magazine: The Kobal Collection, Rex Features and Getty Images.

Front cover photos courtesy: Everett Collection & Globe Photos/Rex Features, Photoshot & Terry O'Neill/Getty Images.

The authors also wish to thank Sir Roger Moore (for *The Saint* images), producer Euan Lloyd (for the *Shalako* images), Tim Greaves, Darren Allison, Mike Siegel, Kevin Wilkinson, Ernest Farino and Andrew Boyle and Gareth Owen of www.bondstars.com for supplying images from their personal collections.

Grateful acknowledgement is made to the following production companies, studios and distributors whose stills, posters and other advertising material illustrate this book for the purposes of publicity and review: Associated British-Pathe, American International Pictures, Amicus, Amsterdam Film, Anglo-Amalgamated, Arena Productions, Artistes Associes, Associated British Pictures, Avco Embassy Pictures, Brent Walker, British Lion Film Corporation, Cambist, Cinema Center Films, Cinematografica Associati, Cineriz, Cocinor, Colorama, Columbia Pictures, Compagnia Cinematografica Champion, Conquest Productions, CUA, Da Ma Produzione, Dania Film, Dimitri De Grunwald Production, Dino de Laurentiis Cinematografica, Documento Film, Emaus Films S.A., EMI, Epee Cinematografica, Erato Films, Eve Productions, Les Films Ariane, Les Films Concordia, Les Films Corona, Les Filmes Marceau, Filmsonor, Francos Films, Galatea Film, Gibshell, Grand Films, Hallmark, Hammer Film Productions, Hesperia Films S.A., Intercontinental, ITC, Jadran Film, Jolly Film, Kingsley International Pictures, K-Tel, Lisa-Film, L.T. Films Inc, Marianne Productions, Medusa Produzione, MGM, MGM Television, Miracle Films, Mirisch G-E Productions, New World Pictures, Nouvelles Editions, Orphée Productions, P.A.C., Parafrance Films, Pad-Ram Ent, Paramount Pictures, PEA, Producciones Benito Perojo, Rank, RKO, Sebastian Films, Selenia Cinematografica, Seven Stars Cinematographica, Sofradis, Sunnymede Film Productions, Tigon Pictures, Trinacra Films, Twentieth Century Fox, United Artists, Universal International, Vides, Warner Bros, Watchgrove Films and World Film Services.

James Bond Aston Martin DB5. With Lee Pfeiffer, he has co-authored the best-selling book *The Essential James Bond* as well as three books for Twentieth Century Fox: *The Great Fox War Movies* and histories of *The Sound of Music* and the *Planet of the Apes* series. Worrall resides in Dorset, England, near the New Forest.

In addition to the titles **Lee Pfeiffer** has written with Dave Worrall, he has also authored books on the careers of Clint Eastwood, Tom Hanks, Sean Connery and Harrison Ford, as well as *The Complete Idiots Guide to Classic Movies*. As editor-in-chief and co-publisher of *Cinema Retro* magazine, Pfeiffer has hosted international film events at a variety of venues, including the legendary Players club in New York City. He has also taught classes about

David Barraclough, our editor at Omnibus Press, whose personal involvement and dedication to this project resulted in the book far exceeding our expectations. However, the drinks at The Groucho Club, next time, are *still* on you, David!

We would also like to thank the following ladies who appear in this book. We have been fortunate to get to know them and greatly appreciate their providing the inspiration for this project: Madeline Smith, Valerie Leon, Caroline Munro, Shirley Anne-Field, Martine Beswick, Margaret Nolan, Britt Ekland, Shirley Eaton, Elke Sommer, Luciana Paluzzi, Ursula Andress and not forgetting Claudia Cardinale.

Finally, we would like to dedicate this book to another friend we came to respect and admire: the late, incomparable Ingrid Pitt.

Above left: Authors Dave Worrall (right) and Lee Pfeiffer with Claudia Cardinale at the VIP party to launch the *Once Upon A Time in Italy.... the Western Films of Sergio Leone* exhibition at the Autry Center, Los Angeles, 2005.

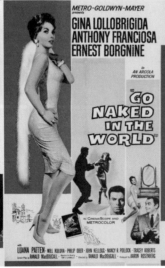